HARRIS COUNTY PUBLIC LIBRARY

3 4028 07386 2683

WITHDRAWN

D1404944

The Right to Privacy

The Right to Privacy

By David L. Hudson Jr.

SERIES EDITOR
Alan Marzilli, M.A., J.D.

CHELSEA HOUSE
PUBLISHERS
An imprint of Infobase Publishing

The Right to Privacy

Chelsea House
An imprint of Infobase Publishing
132 West 31st Street
New York, NY 10001

Library of Congress Cataloging-in-Publication Data

Hudson, David L., 1969–
 The right to privacy / by David L. Hudson.
 p. cm. — (Point/counterpoint)
 Includes bibliographical references and index.
 ISBN 978-1-60413-507-7 (hardcover)
 1. Privacy, Right of—United States. I. Title. II. Series.
 KF1262.H83 2009
 342.7308'58—dc22
                                    2009015015

Series design by Keith Trego
Cover design by Takeshi Takahashi

Printed in the United States of America

Bang EJB 10 9 8 7 6 5 4 3 2 1

This book is printed on acid-free paper.

All links and Web addresses were checked and verified to be correct at the time of publication. Because of the dynamic nature of the Web, some addresses and links may have changed since publication and may no longer be valid.

Alan Marzilli, M.A., J.D.
Birmingham, Alabama

The POINT/COUNTERPOINT series offers the reader a greater understanding of some of the most controversial issues in contemporary American society—issues such as capital punishment, immigration, gay rights, and gun control. We have looked for the most contemporary issues and have included topics—such as the controversies surrounding "blogging"—that we could not have imagined when the series began.

In each volume, the author has selected an issue of particular importance and set out some of the key arguments on both sides of the issue. Why study both sides of the debate? Maybe you have yet to make up your mind on an issue, and the arguments presented in the book will help you to form an opinion. More likely, however, you will already have an opinion on many of the issues covered by the series. There is always the chance that you will change your opinion after reading the arguments for the other side. But even if you are firmly committed to an issue—for example, school prayer or animal rights—reading both sides of the argument will help you to become a more effective advocate for your cause. By gaining an understanding of opposing arguments, you can develop answers to those arguments.

Perhaps more importantly, listening to the other side sometimes helps you see your opponent's arguments in a more human way. For example, Sister Helen Prejean, one of the nation's most visible opponents of capital punishment, has been deeply affected by her interactions with the families of murder victims. By seeing the families' grief and pain, she understands much better why people support the death penalty, and she is able to carry out her advocacy with a greater sensitivity to the needs and beliefs of death penalty supporters.

The books in the series include numerous features that help the reader to gain a greater understanding of the issues. Real-life examples illustrate the human side of the issues. Each chapter also includes excerpts from relevant laws, court cases, and other material, which provide a better foundation for understanding the arguments. The volumes contain citations to relevant sources of law and information, and an appendix guides the reader through the basics of legal research, both on the Internet and in the library. Today, through free Web sites, it is easy to access legal documents, and these books might give you ideas for your own research.

Studying the issues covered by the POINT/COUNTERPOINT series is more than an academic activity. The issues described in the books affect all of us as citizens. They are the issues that today's leaders debate and tomorrow's leaders will decide. While all of the issues covered in the POINT/COUNTERPOINT series are controversial today, and will remain so for the foreseeable future, it is entirely possible that the reader might one day play a central role in resolving the debate. Today it might seem that some debates—such as capital punishment and abortion—will never be resolved.

However, our nation's history is full of debates that seemed as though they never would be resolved, and many of the issues are now well settled—at least on the surface. In the nineteenth century, abolitionists met with widespread resistance to their efforts to end slavery. Ultimately, the controversy threatened the union, leading to the Civil War between the northern and southern states. Today, while a public debate over the merits of slavery would be unthinkable, racism persists in many aspects of society.

Similarly, today nobody questions women's right to vote. Yet at the beginning of the twentieth century, suffragists fought public battles for women's voting rights, and it was not until the passage of the Nineteenth Amendment in 1920 that the legal right of women to vote was established nationwide.

What makes an issue controversial? Often, controversies arise when most people agree that there is a problem but disagree about the best way to solve it. There is little argument that poverty is a major problem in the United States, especially in inner cities and rural areas. Yet, people disagree vehemently about the best way to address the problem. To some, the answer is social programs, such as welfare, food stamps, and public housing. However, many argue that such subsidies encourage dependence on government benefits while unfairly penalizing those who work and pay taxes, and that the real solution is to require people to support themselves.

American society is in a constant state of change, and sometimes modern practices clash with what many consider to be "traditional values," which are often rooted in conservative political views or religious beliefs. Many blame high crime rates, and problems such as poverty, illiteracy, and drug use on the breakdown of the traditional family structure of a married mother and father raising their children. Since the "sexual revolution" of the 1960s and 1970s, sparked in part by the widespread availability of the birth control pill, marriage rates have declined, and the number of children born outside of marriage has increased. The sexual revolution led to controversies over birth control, sex education, and other issues, most prominently abortion. Similarly, the gay rights movement has been challenged as a threat to traditional values. While many gay men and lesbians want to have the same right to marry and raise families as heterosexuals, many politicians and others have challenged gay marriage and adoption as a threat to American society.

Sometimes, new technology raises issues that we have never faced before, and society disagrees about the best solution. Are people free to swap music online, or does this violate the copyright laws that protect songwriters and musicians' ownership of the music that they create? Should scientists use "genetic engineering" to create new crops that are resistant to disease and pests and produce more food, or is it too risky to use a laboratory to create plants that nature never intended? Modern medicine has continued to increase the average lifespan—which is now 77 years, up from under 50 years at the beginning of the twentieth century—but many people are now choosing to die in comfort rather than living with painful ailments in their later years. For doctors, this presents an ethical dilemma: should they allow their patients to die? Should they assist patients in ending their own lives painlessly?

Perhaps the most controversial issues are those that implicate a Constitutional right. The Bill of Rights—the first 10 Amendments to the U.S. Constitution—spells out some of the most fundamental rights that distinguish our democracy from other nations with fewer freedoms. However, the sparsely worded document is open to interpretation, with each side saying that the Constitution is on their side. The Bill of Rights was meant to protect individual liberties; however, the needs of some individuals clash with society's needs. Thus, the Constitution often serves as a battleground between individuals and government officials seeking to protect society in some way. The First Amendment's guarantee of "freedom of speech" leads to some very difficult questions. Some forms of expression—such as burning an American flag—lead to public outrage, but are protected by the First Amendment. Other types of expression that most people find objectionable—such as child pornography—are not protected by the Constitution. The question is not only where to draw the line, but whether drawing lines around constitutional rights threatens our liberty.

The Bill of Rights raises many other questions about individual rights and societal "good." Is a prayer before a high school football game an "establishment of religion" prohibited by the First Amendment? Does the Second Amendment's promise of "the right to bear arms" include concealed handguns? Does stopping and frisking someone standing on a known drug corner constitute "unreasonable search and seizure" in violation of the Fourth Amendment? Although the U.S. Supreme Court has the ultimate authority in interpreting the U.S. Constitution, its answers do not always satisfy the public. When a group of nine people—sometimes by a five-to-four vote—makes a decision that affects hundreds of millions of others, public outcry can be expected. For example, the Supreme Court's 1973 ruling in *Roe v. Wade* that abortion is protected by the Constitution did little to quell the debate over abortion.

Whatever the root of the controversy, the books in the POINT/ COUNTERPOINT series seek to explain to the reader the origins of the debate, the current state of the law, and the arguments on either side of the debate. Our hope in creating this series is that readers will be better informed about the issues facing not only our politicians, but all of our nation's citizens, and become more actively involved in resolving these debates, as voters, concerned citizens, journalists, or maybe even elected officials.

Technology has brought us more and more effective ways of gathering and storing information. We can conduct research instantly and easily, find people, and educate ourselves about health, personal finances, and many other important topics. Such availability of information also creates concerns about the protection of our privacy. A simple mistake made in one's youth might be carried forward into the future in many ways, from public records to photos or even video posted online.

This volume looks at how the law of privacy has evolved to keep pace with technology. While wiretaps were once considered controversial, government surveillance now can include satellite photography, interception of e-mail, analysis of public records using sophisticated software, and even infrared scans of private homes. Proponents say such measures are needed to protect our safety in an age of terrorism, but privacy advocates are gravely concerned. Also of concern to many is the way news outlets gather information. Fewer people are getting their news from traditional sources like newspapers and more from blogs and tabloid-type Web sites that do not always play by traditional notions of journalistic restraint. A final area examined in this installment of POINT-COUNTERPOINT concerns the privacy of people at work. Students at school may expect their online and offline activities to be monitored, but must adult employees expect the same scrutiny?

An Overview of the Right to Privacy

The makers of our Constitution undertook to secure conditions favorable to the pursuit of happiness. They recognized the signifi-cance of man's spiritual nature, of his feelings and of his intellect. They knew that only a part of the pain, pleasure and satisfactions of life are to be found in material things. They sought to protect Americans in their beliefs, their thoughts, their emotions and their sensations. They conferred, as against the government, the right to be let alone—the most comprehensive of rights and the right most valued by civilized men.

—Justice Louis Brandeis in *Olmstead v. United States* (1928)[1]

Consider the most important rights individuals possess in a free society. Among these, people enjoy the right to express their thoughts, practice their religion, and make fundamental decisions about how to live their lives. We cherish the right to

Louis D. Brandeis (1874-1941) served as a U.S. Supreme Court justice from 1916 to 1939. Before becoming one of the most influential figures ever to serve on the high court, he and his law partner Samuel Warren penned an important law review article on the right to privacy. As a Supreme Court justice, Brandeis issued case opinions that are considered among the greatest defenses of freedom of speech and the right to privacy ever written.

be treated equally and not face discrimination because of our race, religion, or sex. Foremost among all fundamental rights, however, might be what Thomas Cooley and Louis Brandeis termed the "the right to be let alone." Brandeis called it the "most comprehensive of rights." We refer to it as privacy.

The word privacy comes from the Latin word *privatus*, which means set apart and belonging to oneself. Privatus is the opposite of *publicus*, which refers to being in public or in the community. People generallly do not want their entire lives or their personal information made public; rather they want to keep much of their lives private. We do not want the government or other people invading our individual spheres of liberty, whether we are home, in public, on the job, or anywhere else.

It is difficult to define privacy. Any definition of privacy would need to encompass all aspects of wanting to be let alone. Jim Harper, the editor of Privacilla.org, defines privacy as "a state of affairs or condition having to do with the amount of personal information that is known to others."[2] Sissela Bok referred to it as "the condition of being protected from unwanted access by others—either physical access, personal information or attention."[3]

Legal scholar Ken Gormley writes: "Commentators have stumbled over privacy, and have failed to agree upon an acceptable definition, because they have generally focused on privacy as a philosophical or moral concept . . . while wholly ignoring privacy as a legal concept."[4] Gormley argues that privacy is best understood by examining the different legal sources on the subject, including privacy in tort law, in the Fourth and the First Amendments, fundamental privacy, and state constitutional law privacy.[5]

Another similar, but simpler, way to define legal privacy is by placing it in the context of one of three groups: common-law privacy, constitutional privacy, and statutory privacy. *Common law* refers to judge-made law, not based specifically on the Constitution or in a law or statute. Common-law privacy refers to privacy as a tort—a civil cause of action in which one person sues another for monetary damages. Constitutional privacy refers to the protection of privacy that is derived from the U.S. Constitution (specifically the Bill of Rights) and various state constitutions. Finally, federal and state legislators can pass laws, or statutes, that protect privacy.

Tort-law, or Common-law Privacy

One of the main ways our privacy is safeguarded is through the law of torts. Our courts are generally divided into criminal and civil (noncriminal) courts. Civil cases involve a plaintiff, who seeks either money or a specific course of action from a defendant. Traditionally, civil cases involved either contracts (agreements between the parties) or torts (some kind of wrongdoing or harm). A tort is a civil wrong, defined as one party engaging in socially unreasonable conduct that causes another party damages. A person who commits a tort is called a tortfeasor. The simplest example is a car accident that injures someone or that causes damages to his or her car. Invasion of privacy, however, is also a tort. For many years tort law did not recognize a cause of action—or legal claim—for privacy. The law was concerned only with protecting people from such things as assault, battery, or false imprisonment. In the late nineteenth century, two attorneys based in Boston changed that forever. They were Samuel Warren and Louis Brandeis.

It began when Warren became upset at local press coverage of Beacon Hill parties. According to some sources, Warren was angry about reports describing his daughter's attendance at a party, while others believed his ire was reserved for the press's inclusion of a Beacon Hill party guest list. Whatever the source of his frustration, Warren believed that the so-called "yellow press" was overstepping its bounds. Together with his law partner Louis Brandeis, who later became a U.S. Supreme Court justice, Warren wrote a landmark law review article, "The Right to Privacy," published in the *Harvard Law Review*.[6]

Warren and Brandeis reasoned that the law should evolve to protect people from emotional harm, in addition to protecting them, as it already did, from physical harm. They also noted that society was changing as the modern world became more industrialized. They explained: "The intensity and complexity of life, attendant upon advancing civilization, have rendered necessary some retreat from the world, and man . . . has become more sensitive to publicity, so that solitude and privacy have become more essential to the individual."[7] They added that "the common law secures to each individual the right of determining, ordinarily, to what extent his thoughts, sentiments, and emotions shall be communicated to others."[8] Brandeis and Warren then concluded:

> Recent inventions and business methods call attention to the next step which must be taken for the protection of the person, and for securing to the individual what Judge Cooley calls the "right to be let alone." Instantaneous photographs and newspaper enterprise have invaded the sacred precincts of private and domestic life; and numerous mechanical devices threaten to make good the prediction that "what is whispered in the closet shall be proclaimed from the house-tops."[9]

According to Warren and Brandeis, "the press is overstepping in every direction the obvious bounds of propriety and decency." They were concerned about two chief evils: "numerous mechanical devices" and the overreaching conduct of the press.[10]

Gradually, beginning in the twentieth century, courts started to recognize invasion of privacy as a legitimate tort claim. The legal landscape was far from clear, however, as courts in different states adopted different types of privacy claims. Uniformity in common-law privacy tort law began in 1960, when the legal scholar William Prosser wrote an influential law review article in which he characterized the invasion of privacy as four separate sub-torts: intrusion; public disclosure of private facts; false light;

and appropriation.[11] In their book *The Right to Privacy*, Caroline Kennedy and Ellen Alderman noted the evolution of privacy: "If the privacy tort was born in 1890, then it came of age in 1960, again because of a legal article."

Intrusion Upon Physical Solitude

The intrusion tort best represents the commonly understood meaning of privacy. As the California Supreme Court wrote in 1998, it is "perhaps the one that best captures the common understanding of an 'invasion of privacy.'" An influential summary of tort laws, *The Restatement (Second) of Torts* §652(B), defines intrusion as follows: "One who intentionally intrudes, physically or otherwise, upon the solitude or seclusion of another or his private affairs or concerns, is subject to liability to the other for invasion of privacy, if the intrusion would be highly offensive to a reasonable person." This is the tort that applies to the very aggressive newsgathering practices of paparazzi-style photographers, for example, and will be examined in more detail in later chapters.

Public Disclosure of Private Facts

This privacy sub-tort refers to the disclosure to the public by an individual of very private information about another person. The *Restatement* defines this tort as: "One who gives publicity to a matter concerning the private life of another is subject to liability to the other for invasion of his privacy, if the matter publicized is of a kind that: (a) would be highly offensive to a reasonable person, and (b) is not of legitimate concern to the public."[12] These public-disclosure-of-private-facts cases often turn on whether the information released is considered to be material that is "newsworthy." Some consider these claims to be the most controversial because they involve punishing the media for the release of even truthful information.

The U.S. Supreme Court in several cases has determined that the First Amendment protected the media from publishing even highly sensitive information, particularly if the information came from a public record. In *Cox Broadcasting Co. v. Cohn*, the high court ruled that the press could not be punished for truthfully reporting that the plaintiff's daughter was a rape victim when the media obtained the information from a public record. The Court wrote that "the First and Fourteenth Amendments command nothing less than that the States may not impose sanctions on the publication of truthful information contained in official court records open to public inspection." [13]

False Light

False-light invasion of privacy is similar to defamation. It refers to situations in which a party publishes information about a person or persons that places them in a false light or represents them in misleading ways. For example, a television station runs a program about the problems of street-walking prostitution and shows photographs of a woman walking down the street. Unless the woman is a prostitute, she has been placed in a false light.

The *Restatement (Second) of Torts* defines false light as follows: "One who gives publicity to a matter concerning another that places the other before the public in a false light is subject to liability to the other for invasion of his privacy, if: (a) the false light in which the other was placed would be highly offensive to a reasonable person, and (b) the actor had knowledge of or acted in reckless disregard as to the falsity of the publicized matter and the false light in which the other would be placed." [14]

Appropriation

The appropriation tort prohibits someone from using someone else's name, likeness, or personality for advertising, a commercial purpose, or similar use. The law defines this tort as: "One who appropriates to his own use or benefit the name or likeness of another is subject to liability to the other for invasion of privacy." [15] For example, if a manufacturer advertises its basketballs with pictures and images of Michael Jordan without his per-

FROM THE BENCH

Cox Broadcasting Co. v. Cohn, 420 U.S. 469, 491–492 (1975)

In this sphere of collision between claims of privacy and those of the free press, the interests on both sides are plainly rooted in the traditions and significant concerns of our society. Rather than address the broader question whether truthful publications may ever be subjected to civil or criminal liability consistently with the First and Fourteenth Amendments, or to put it another way, whether the State may ever define and protect an area of privacy free from unwanted publicity in the press, it is appropriate to focus on the narrower interface between press and privacy that this case presents, namely, whether the State may impose sanctions on the accurate publication of the name of a rape victim obtained from public records—more specifically, from judicial records which are maintained in connection with a public prosecution and which themselves are open to public inspection. We are convinced that the State may not do so.

In the first place, in a society in which each individual has but limited time and resources with which to observe at first hand the operations of his government, he relies necessarily upon the press to bring to him in convenient form the facts of those operations. Great responsibility is accordingly placed upon the news media to report fully and accurately the proceedings of government, and official records and documents open to the public are the basic data of governmental operations. Without the information provided by the press most of us and many of our representatives would be unable to vote intelligently or to register opinions on the administration of government generally. With respect to judicial proceedings in particular, the function of the press serves to guarantee the fairness of trials and to bring to bear the beneficial effects of public scrutiny upon the administration of justice....

Appellee has claimed in this litigation that the efforts of the press have infringed his right to privacy by broadcasting to the world the fact that his daughter was a rape victim. The commission of crime, prosecutions resulting from it, and judicial proceedings arising from the prosecutions, however, are without question events of legitimate concern to the public and consequently fall within the responsibility of the press to report the operations of government.

mission, the company has appropriated Jordan's image and has violated his privacy rights.

Constitutional Privacy

Although neither the U.S. Constitution nor the Bill of Rights mentions the word "privacy," several constitutional amendments protect aspects of privacy. The First Amendment—best known for protecting freedom of expression and religion—sometimes protects privacy interests. An example of this occurred in 1958, when the U.S. Supreme Court ruled in *NAACP v. Alabama* that the state of Alabama could not force the National Association for the Advanced of Colored People (NAACP) to disclose its membership lists.[16] The Court recognized that the NAACP members had a right to privacy that protected them from harassment.

The Third Amendment also protects individual privacy, in that it prohibits the government from quartering troops in individuals' homes. This ensures the privacy of families by preventing them from having to open up their homes to the government and members of the military.

The amendment that most directly affects privacy rights is the Fourth Amendment, which provides:

> The right of the people to be secure in their persons, houses, papers, and effects, against unreasonable searches and seizures, shall not be violated, and no Warrants shall issue, but upon probable cause, supported by Oath or affirmation, and particularly describing the place to be searched, and the persons or things to be seized.

In *Mapp v. Ohio* (1961), the U.S. Supreme Court noted that the Fourth Amendment protects "the right to privacy, no less important than any other right carefully and particularly reserved to the people."[17] It protects individuals from "unreasonable searches and seizures" by government officials. It prohibits so-called general warrants, which fail to particularly describe the objects of the search. The framers of the Constitution had wished to avoid the pitfalls caused by "writs of assistance," which were general-type warrants that British officials used to search and seize colonial property and effects.

The Fourth Amendment also has modern-day relevance, particularly as technological advances give government officials greater ability to conduct surveillance and search into more aspects of people's lives. A prominent example of the U.S. government's expanded capabilities is a part of the law known as the Providing Appropriate Tools Required to Intercept and Obstruct Terrorism, better known by its acronym, the PATRIOT Act. Fourth Amendment scholars Otis H. Stephens and Richard Glenn write: "Currently, the most serious threat to Fourth Amendment rights is posed by legislation adopted by Congress in the aftermath of the terrorist attacks of September 11, 2001."[18] They and others have discussed provisions of the PATRIOT Act that greatly increase the government's powers of surveillance, which include "sneak-and-peak" searches and searches conducted ostensibly for foreign intelligence but applied to domestic information as well.[19]

The Fifth Amendment, particularly the Self-Incrimination Clause, protects individuals from having to testify or give evidence against themselves to the government or in a court of law. In 1965, in the case of *Griswold v. Connecticut*, a case about marital privacy and the use of contraceptives, Justice William O. Douglas wrote that "the Fifth Amendment in its Self-Incrimination Clause enables the citizen to create a zone of privacy which government may not force him to surrender to his detriment."[20]

The Ninth Amendment also can be interpreted as providing protection for privacy because it states that "the enumeration in the Constitution, of certain rights, shall not be construed to deny or disparage others retained by the people." In plain English, this means that the Constitution gives people more rights than those listed (or enumerated) in the Bill of Rights. Justice Arthur Goldberg emphasized the importance of the Ninth Amendment in his concurring opinion in *Griswold v. Connecticut*: "The Ninth Amendment simply shows the intent of the Constitution's authors that other fundamental personal rights should not be denied such protection or disparaged in any other way simply because they are not specifically listed in the first eight constitutional amendments."[21]

Additionally, the Fourteenth Amendment provides that "no state shall deprive any person of life, liberty, or property without due process of law." This means that the government must not act arbitrarily or unreasonably when it interferes with a person's freedom to act as he or she chooses. In *Roe v. Wade* (1973), the U.S. Supreme Court interpreted the Fourteenth Amendment's "liberty" interest to protect a woman's right of privacy in her reproductive health choices—in that particular case, the choice of an abortion. More recently, in the 2003 decision *Lawrence v. Texas*, the U.S. Supreme Court ruled that the state of Texas could not criminalize certain sexual acts committed in the privacy of the home because such a step violated liberty and privacy rights protected by the due-process clause of the Fourteenth Amendment.[22]

All of these constitutional amendments to the U.S. Constitution—the First, Third, Fourth, Fifth, Ninth, and Fourteenth—protect privacy in certain circumstances and ways. There are, however, other constitutions in our legal system: Every state in the Union has its own constitution. Under basic constitutional law principles, a state is free to interpret its own state constitution to provide greater protection than the U.S. Constitution provides. Thus, individuals may have privacy rights under federal and state constitutions.

Statutory Rights of Privacy

When considering privacy, many people believe it concerns common-law or constitutional privacy. They think of the intrusive paparazzi invading a person's private space or an overly

(continues on page 25)

Video Privacy Protection Act of 1988

18 U.S.C. 2710

(a) Definitions.—For purposes of this section—

(1) the term "consumer" means any renter, purchaser, or subscriber of goods or services from a video tape service provider;

(2) the term "ordinary course of business" means only debt collection activities, order fulfillment, request processing, and the transfer of ownership;

(3) the term "personally identifiable information" includes information which identifies a person as having requested or obtained specific video materials or services from a video tape service provider; and

(4) the term "video tape service provider" means any person, engaged in the business, in or affecting interstate or foreign commerce, of rental, sale, or delivery of prerecorded video cassette tapes or similar audio visual materials, or any person or other entity to whom a disclosure is made under subparagraph (D) or (E) of subsection (b)(2), but only with respect to the information contained in the disclosure.

(b) Video Tape Rental and Sale Records.—

(1) A video tape service provider who knowingly discloses, to any person, personally identifiable information concerning any consumer of such provider shall be liable to the aggrieved person for the relief provided in subsection (d).

(2) A video tape service provider may disclose personally identifiable information concerning any consumer—

(A) to the consumer;

(B) to any person with the informed, written consent of the consumer given at the time the disclosure is sought;

(C) to a law enforcement agency pursuant to a warrant issued under the Federal Rules of Criminal Procedure, an equivalent State warrant, a grand jury subpoena, or a court order;

(D) to any person if the disclosure is solely of the names and addresses of consumers and if—

(i) the video tape service provider has provided the consumer with the opportunity, in a clear and conspicuous manner, to prohibit such disclosure; and

(ii) the disclosure does not identify the title, description, or subject matter of any video tapes or other audio visual material; however, the subject matter of such materials may be disclosed if the disclosure is for the exclusive use of marketing goods and services directly to the consumer;

(E) to any person if the disclosure is incident to the ordinary course of business of the video tape service provider; or

(F) pursuant to a court order, in a civil proceeding upon a showing of compelling need for the information that cannot be accommodated by any other means, if—

(i) the consumer is given reasonable notice, by the person seeking the disclosure, of the court proceeding relevant to the issuance of the court order; and

(ii) the consumer is afforded the opportunity to appear and contest the claim of the person seeking the disclosure.

If an order is granted pursuant to subparagraph (C) or (F), the court shall impose appropriate safeguards against unauthorized disclosure.

(3) Court orders authorizing disclosure under subparagraph (C) shall issue only with prior notice to the consumer and only if the law enforcement agency shows that there is probable cause to believe that the records or other information sought are relevant to a legitimate law enforcement inquiry. In the case of a State government authority, such a court order shall not issue if prohibited by the law of such State. A court issuing an order pursuant to this section, on a motion made promptly by the video tape service provider, may quash or modify such order if the information or records requested are unreasonably voluminous in nature or if compliance with such order otherwise would cause an unreasonable burden on such provider.

(continues on page 24)

(continued from page 23)

(c) Civil Action.—

(1) Any person aggrieved by any act of a person in violation of this section may bring a civil action in a United States district court.

(2) The court may award—

(A) actual damages but not less than liquidated damages in an amount of $2,500;

(B) punitive damages;

(C) reasonable attorneys' fees and other litigation costs reasonably incurred; and

(D) such other preliminary and equitable relief as the court determines to be appropriate.

(3) No action may be brought under this subsection unless such action is begun within 2 years from the date of the act complained of or the date of discovery.

(4) No liability shall result from lawful disclosure permitted by this section.

(d) Personally Identifiable Information.—Personally identifiable information obtained in any manner other than as provided in this section shall not be received in evidence in any trial, hearing, arbitration, or other proceeding in or before any court, grand jury, department, officer, agency, regulatory body, legislative committee, or other authority of the United States, a State, or a political subdivision of a State.

(e) Destruction of Old Records.—A person subject to this section shall destroy personally identifiable information as soon as practicable, but no later than one year from the date the information is no longer necessary for the purpose for which it was collected and there are no pending requests or orders for access to such information under subsection (b)(2) or (c)(2) or pursuant to a court order.

(f) Preemption.—The provisions of this section preempt only the provisions of State or local law that require disclosure prohibited by this section.

(continued from page 21)
aggressive law enforcement official engaged in an unreasonable search or seizure. Common law and Constitution, however, are not the only sources that protect privacy interests. Various laws have been enacted to ensure privacy.

Numerous federal laws exist to protect the privacy of certain communication and information, such as student, medical, video, and driver's license records. For example, in 1974, Congress passed the Family Educational Rights and Privacy Act, or FERPA, to provide confidentiality for student records.[23] In 1978, Congress passed the Right to Financial Privacy Act to provide more protection for consumers' bank records from government intrusiveness.[24] Two years later, Congress passed the Privacy Protection Act of 1980 to give more privacy protection to newspapers. Lawmakers passed the law in direct response to the U.S. Supreme Court decision in *Zurcher v. Stanford Daily* (1978), which upheld an intrusive governmental search of a student newsroom.[25]

In 1986, Congress passed the Electronic Communications Privacy Act to provide greater protection for the privacy of all forms of electronic transmissions, including video, text, and data.[26] Two years later Congress passed the Video Privacy Protection of 1988, after the video-rental records of failed U.S. Supreme Court nominee Robert Bork were released during his confirmation hearings.[27] In 1994, Congress passed the Driver Privacy Protection Act to prohibit departments of motor vehicles from giving out drivers' home addresses and other personal information.[28] The impetus for this bill came from the murder of a television actress by a deranged fan who obtained her home address from her driving records.

In 1996, Congress passed the Health Insurance Portability and Accountability Act (HIPAA) to protect individuals' medical records. Other federal statutes that provide privacy protection include the Fair Credit Reporting Act, the Privacy Act of 1974, the Identity Theft and Assumption Deterrence Act, and the Telephone Consumer Protection Act.

Privacy Controversies Examined in This Book

Among the numerous privacy controversies facing the United States, this book examines in detail three of the highest-profile issues that resonate in today's society. The first concerns government surveillance. In seeking out possible enemies, is the government acting as an intrusive Big Brother invading privacy rights or is it employing a necessary crime-combating tool in an age of global terrorism? The second concerns electronic monitoring in the workplace. Proponents of such monitoring insist that employers must deal with "cyberslackers," employee espionage, lowered levels of productivity, and potential legal problems associated with unfettered and unchecked employee communications. Opponents believe it is a clear example of employers violating their employees' privacy. The third examines which newsgathering activities and techniques may constitute gross intrusions and invasions of common-law privacy and which, perhaps even intrusive or deceptive ones, should receive a healthy degree of First Amendment protection.

Governmental Surveillance Often Infringes on Individuals' Fourth Amendment Rights

Winston Smith objected to a government that instituted surveillance on him and his fellow citizens as part of its totalitarian grip on society. "The Party" engaged in all sorts of duplicitous activities in order to keep its stranglehold on the public. It was unable to accomplish these without surveillance. As you may know, Winston Smith is not a real person; he was the protagonist in George Orwell's nightmarish book *1984*. Unfortunately, the Big Brother of the novel is not only a fictional creation; it is a present-day reality. Governments around the globe engage in constant surveillance of their populaces. Surveillance is omnipresent. Such surveillance, it is claimed, is necessary to combat crime and terrorism. The question, however, is whether it is indeed necessary to give up liberty for a bit of supposed security.

The Fourth Amendment protects people's reasonable expectations of privacy.

The Fourth Amendment does not contain the word "privacy," but the amendment is designed to safeguard individuals from invasive government action. It prohibits the government from conducting unreasonable searches and seizures that compromise a person's privacy. Ellen Alderman and Caroline Kennedy explain that the Fourth Amendment "is the most direct constitutional safeguard for privacy."[1]

Numerous laws, programs, and policies threaten individuals' privacy rights under the Fourth Amendment. One of the most worrisome examples is government surveillance by video, electronic, or other technological means. The U.S. Supreme Court has clearly recognized that surveillance by government officials could constitute an unreasonable search and seizure within the meaning of the Fourth Amendment. "There is a constant tension between surveillance powers sought by law enforcement and the privacy-protecting rights enjoyed by Americans," writes Jim Harper. "The rules laid down by the Constitution, chiefly in the Fourth Amendment, demarcate the line between appropriate and inappropriate surveillance."[2]

The U.S. Supreme Court has recognized that government surveillance can violate the Fourth Amendment.

Initially, the U.S. Supreme Court did not find that surveillance violated the Fourth Amendment. In 1928, the high court ruled in the case of bootlegger Roy Olmstead that federal agents could record private conversations of Olmstead and others to show that they were violating the National Prohibition Act of 1920, which outlawed the sale, manufacturing, and trafficking of alcohol. (The law was repealed in 1933.) Olmstead contended that the government's secret recordings of his conversations violated his Fourth Amendment rights. The Court, however, rejected his constitutional claim in a 5-4 decision, reasoning that the Fourth

Amendment required a physical, tangible invasion—such as federal agents ransacking a home looking for evidence.[3]

Justice Louis Brandeis, however, wrote a passionate dissenting opinion that warned about government encroachments on privacy. He noted that the framers of the Constitution sought to protect the individual from the invasive arm of government:

> They sought to protect Americans in their beliefs, their thoughts, their emotions and their sensations. They conferred, as against the government, the right to be let alone—the most comprehensive of rights and the right most valued by civilized men. To protect that right, every unjustifiable intrusion by the government upon the privacy of the individual, whatever the means

FROM THE BENCH

Olmstead v. United States, 277 U.S. 438, 465-466 (1928) (majority opinion)

Congress may, of course, protect the secrecy of telephone messages by making them, when intercepted, inadmissible in evidence in federal criminal trials, by direct legislation, and thus depart from the common law of evidence. But the courts may not adopt such a policy by attributing an enlarged and unusual meaning to the Fourth Amendment. The reasonable view is that one who installs in his house a telephone instrument with connecting wires intends to project his voice to those quite outside, and that the wires beyond his house, and messages while passing over them, are not within the protection of the Fourth Amendment. Here those who intercepted the projected voices were not in the house of either party to the conversation.

Neither the cases we have cited nor any of the many federal decisions brought to our attention hold the Fourth Amendment to have been violated as against a defendant, unless there has been an official search and seizure of his person or such a seizure of his papers or his tangible material effects or an actual physical invasion of his house "or curtilage" for the purpose of making a seizure.

employed, must be deemed a violation of the Fourth Amendment.[4]

Brandeis's opinion was vindicated when the Supreme Court overruled its decision in the *Olmstead* case nearly 40 years later in *Katz v. United States* (1967).[5] The new case involved the government's tapping of a public telephone to confirm suspicions they had that Charles Katz operated as an illegal gambler. The government did not obtain a warrant, contending that investigators were allowed to tap the phone and conduct surveillance because their actions did not constitute any type of physical invasion. In an opinion by Justice Potter Stewart, the Supreme Court rejected this argument and overruled its *Olmstead* decision:

> The Government's activities in electronically listening to and recording the petitioner's [Charles Katz] words violated the privacy upon which he justifiably relied while using the telephone booth and thus constituted a "search and seizure" within the meaning of the Fourth Amendment.[6]

Stewart concluded in his *Katz* opinion that the police easily could have complied with the Fourth Amendment if they had sought a warrant before conducting their surreptitious surveillance of Charles Katz. They did not; instead they violated his privacy. "Wherever a man may be, he is entitled to know that he will remain free from unreasonable searches and seizures," Stewart wrote. "Because the surveillance here failed to meet that condition, and because it led to the petitioner's conviction, the judgment must be reversed."[7]

While Stewart wrote the majority opinion, it was Justice John Marshall Harlan II who in his concurring opinion created the vital concept that the Fourth Amendment protects people's "reasonable expectation of privacy."

In another 1967 decision, *Berger v. New York*, the U.S. Supreme Court recognized that eavesdropping by government officials could constitute a serious intrusion on individuals' constitutional rights. "Few threats to liberty exist which are greater than that posed by the use of eavesdropping devices," the Court wrote.[8]

The very next year, Congress passed Title III of the Omnibus Crime Control and Safe Streets Act of 1968, a law that required government officials to obtain warrants for surveillance, something federal agents failed to do in the Charles Katz case. In 1978, Congress passed the Foreign Intelligence Surveillance Act (FISA), which required government officials

FROM THE BENCH

Katz v. United States, 389 U.S. 347, 361 (1967) (concurring opinion)

As the Court's opinion states, "the Fourth Amendment protects people, not places." The question, however, is what protection it affords to those people. Generally, as here, the answer to that question requires reference to a "place." My understanding of the rule that has emerged from prior decisions is that there is a twofold requirement, first that a person have exhibited an actual (subjective) expectation of privacy and, second, that the expectation be one that society is prepared to recognize as "reasonable." Thus a man's home is, for most purposes, a place where he expects privacy, but objects, activities, or statements that he exposes to the "plain view" of outsiders are not "protected" because no intention to keep them to himself has been exhibited. On the other hand, conversations in the open would not be protected against being overheard, for the expectation of privacy under the circumstances would be unreasonable.

The critical fact in this case is that "[o]ne who occupies it [a telephone booth], shuts the door behind him, and pays the toll that permits him to place a call is surely entitled to assume" that his conversation is not being intercepted. ... The point is not that the booth is "accessible to the public" at other times, but that it is a temporarily private place whose momentary occupants' expectations of freedom from intrusion are recognized as reasonable.

to obtain warrants before intercepting international communications between U.S. citizens and anyone in the United States if one of the parties to the conversation is believed to be a foreign terrorist. FISA was designed to give the government a legal basis on which to conduct foreign surveillance to deal with national security threats. Both Title III and FISA are examples of the government imposing safeguards before conducting surveillance and violating fundamental Fourth Amendment rights.

People have expectations of privacy even in public places.

Many argue that certain types of surveillance of persons in public—for instance most forms of video surveillance—fail to violate individual privacy because the people are in public view. This ignores people's belief that they should have privacy rights even when they are in public. Most important, people should have the right to remain anonymous when walking or driving in public. The Electronic Privacy Information Center (EPIC) explains that people do have expectations of privacy even in public places. The center argues that "as long as people are conducting themselves in ways that are not seen as extraordinary, they can and do expect privacy."[9]

There are many reasons for society to provide that people should have expectations of privacy even in public places. "At a basic level, those in control of surveillance cameras could zoom in on attractive women or track individuals because of their race," writes legal commentator Jeremy Brown. "At a more sophisticated level, hackers could break into wireless networks and hijack police cameras. License plate readers could link information about the geographic movement of cars to private data like the insurance records of car owners."[10]

People want to have some confidence of privacy in public spaces even given the dramatic increase in technologies that can violate it. Cell-phone cameras and other technological devices can be used for insidious purposes. For example, the proliferation of video voyeurism and "upskirting" statutes arose because some nefarious characters were invading the privacy rights of others. Upskirting refers to the practice of filming women's undergarments while they are walking in public. As the National Center for the Victims of Crime reports, numerous states have passed laws to prohibit such invasive conduct, even if it occurs in public places.[11]

Furthermore, the idea that people can have no expectation of privacy in any public place simply doesn't make sense. "The cost to society and individual autonomy is unacceptably high if we insist that everyone live as if she were being watched or recorded at all times," writes legal commentator Kristin Beasley.[12] She explains that there are serious negative consequences for society if people believe they forfeit their privacy whenever they leave their home.[13] People may have feelings of fear when they engage in such mundane activities as walking their dog down the street, going to the shopping mall, or running daily errands.

Not all surveillance systems have been proven effective.

Many cities have received funding from the U.S. Department of Homeland Security, which has allocated more than $200 million in grants for public camera surveillance programs, like the system considered by the District of Columbia. Yet EPIC has persuasively proven the lack of effectiveness of such systems. EPIC contends that "studies have found that it is more effective to place more officers on the streets than have them watching people on monitors."[14] Marc Rotenberg, head of EPIC, argues that "the benefits of video surveillance systems as a means to reduce crime and deter terrorism have been significantly overstated."[15]

Others agree that the benefits of camera surveillance systems have been greatly overstated. Norm Biale, advocacy coordinator with the American Civil Liberties Union's Technology

Under surveillance

Most Americans support expanded U.S. law enforcement against terrorism, but six months after Sept. 11, their enthusiasm has waned.

Type of surveillance	Sept. 2001	March 2002
More undercover work to penetrate suspicious groups	93%	88%
Face recognition technology to scan for suspected terrorists at public events	86%	81%
Monitoring bank, credit card transactions to trace sources of funds	81%	72%
National ID system for all U.S. citizens	68%	59%
Camera surveillance on streets, in public places	63%	58%
Monitoring cell phones, e-mail to intercept communications	54%	44%
About law enforcers		
Very confident law enforcers will use expanded powers properly	34%	12%

Source: Harris Poll telephone survey of 1,017 U.S. adults, March 13 to 19; 3 percent error margin   Graphic: Pat Carr, Pai   © 2002 KRT

Opinion poll results show that Americans' willingness to tolerate more intrusive police surveillance dropped six months after the September 11, 2001 terrorist attacks.

and Liberty Program, conducted an analysis of various studies of video surveillance from 2000 to 2008. His conclusion from studying the effects of such systems in the United Kingdom and the United States is that "meta-analyses from the UK, along with preliminary findings from the US, indicate strongly that video surveillance has little to no positive impact on crime."[16]

Government surveillance programs in a post-9/11 world show a lack of concern for privacy.

After the terrorist attacks of September 11, 2001 that resulted in the deaths of almost 3,000 people in New York City, near Washington, D.C., and in Shanksville, Pennsylvania, government surveillance increased significantly. President George W. Bush's administration approved a program of warrantless domestic surveillance in order to further national security interests. The Terrorist Surveillance Program conducted by the National Security Agency (NSA) led to a "sea change" in how surveillance was conducted in the United States. The program caused many observers and experts to believe that "the surveillance has stretched, if not crossed, constitutional limits on legal searches."[17] One notable change is that video surveillance has increased since 9/11. Many cities that were not already using surveillance in public places considered doing so to combat the possiblity of another terrorist attack.

In 2008, Congress passed the FISA Amendments Act, which broadened the government's ability to conduct electronic surveillance.[18] This law did away with the old requirement that the government must have suspicion of a particular individual before it could conduct electronic surveillance. "The target could be a human rights activist, a media organization, a geographic region, or even a country," the American Civil Liberties Union warned. "In fact, under the new law the government doesn't have to identify its surveillance targets at all."[19] The ACLU adds that the "extensive academic literature on the subject . . . strongly indicates that video surveillance has no statistically significant effect on crime rates."[20] The ACLU challenged this law in the federal lawsuit *Amnesty International USA v. McConnell*.[21]

Summary

Government surveillance can violate individuals' rights under the Fourth Amendment. People have a reasonable expectation of privacy even when they are in a public place. For the government to constantly observe its citizens' every movement is right out of George Orwell's *1984*. Under the guise of combating crime and fighting terrorism, the United States has allowed for greater public surveillance to the detriment of civil liberties, including the protection from intrusiveness guaranteed by the Constitution. This does not bode well for those who care deeply about the fundamental right of privacy.

Modern Surveillance Provides Necessary Security and Does Not Violate the Fourth Amendment

On Tuesday, September 11, 2001, Mohammed Atta and Abdulaziz al-Omari arrived at an airport in Portland, Maine to travel to Boston. When Atta checked in for his flight, he was flagged by the Computer Assisted Passenger Prescreening System (CAPPS). This system was designed to identify passengers who should be subject to special security measures. The only consequence of this security system was that his bags were held off the plane until he boarded. This had no effect, as we know, on what was to happen. In Boston, Atta and al-Omari boarded a flight bound for Los Angeles, which they then hijacked and crashed into one of the Twin Towers of New York City's World Trade Center. Some of Atta's colleagues in the terrorist group al Qaeda crashed another plane into the other Twin Tower. CAPPS screened several of them. *The 9/11 Commission Report* later found that "the challenge is to see the common framework—an architecture—for an effective screening system."[1] The commission's members stated that they "learned of the pervasive problems of managing and sharing information across a large and unwieldy government that had been built in a different era to confront different dangers."[2]

One lesson of 9/11 was that our country and government had insufficient security measures in place to protect the populace in an age of global terrorism. Legal commentator Julie Hilden explains that face-recognition technology might have deterred the 9/11 attacks. She wrote: "We all remember the airport videotape of Mohammed Atta, the suspected ringleader of the September 11 terrorism attacks: He was caught on camera, and if his face had been on file, he might also have been stopped before the plane he boarded ever took off."[3]

Better and increased surveillance can only help in the constant, vigilant battle against evil in the world. Beyond its use in the war on terror, surveillance can assist in domestic crime that harms countless victims.

Crime not only hurts its victims; it hinders the effective functioning of society. Law enforcement departments lack sufficient manpower to combat the pervasive and insidious reality of crime. The use of technology, however, particularly surveillance tools, increases law enforcement's ability to protect citizens from predators. This enhanced ability occurs at the international, national, state, and local levels.

Surveillance works.

Consider two examples: In the early 1990s, Northampton, England was besieged by a serious crime wave, partly from terrorist activities of the Irish Republican Army (IRA). The city installed a series of security cameras that allowed law enforcement to monitor many public spaces. The results were impressive and dramatic, as the city's crime rate was reduced 57 percent by the mid-1990s. In Tacoma, Washington, the installation of surveillance cameras led to a 38 percent reduction in crime in just one year.[4]

One legal commentator has acknowledged that "the development of surveillance technology, and its late convergence
with state of the art computers, databases, and telecommunica-
tions systems, has dramatically enhanced government's ability
to perform its law enforcement functions."[5] A large network of
surveillance cameras in London enabled law enforcement officials to quickly identify the terrorists who committed the mass-
transit bombings on July 7, 2005.[6]

Government surveillance does not violate the Fourth Amendment.

Government surveillance of suspected wrongdoers seldom violates the Fourth Amendment. In many cases, the government's
actions in installing surveillance devices constitute perfectly
legitimate and effective measures designed to protect the public.
In *United States v. Torres* (1984), agents of the Federal Bureau of
Investigation installed bugs and hidden cameras in an apartment
that was suspected of being a safe house for a clandestine para-
military group called Fuerzas Armadas de Liberacion Nacional
Puertorriquena (FALN). The group was known for using vio-
lence in its efforts to establish independence for Puerto Rico, a
territory of the United States. The Seventh U.S. Circuit Court
of Appeals determined that the government was justified in its
surveillance in part because "the benefits to the public safety are
great, and the costs to personal privacy are modest."[7]

Video surveillance helps to deter crime.

Common sense alone tells us that cameras reduce crime.
Consider the following scenario: A would-be criminal observes
two customers withdrawing money from the ATMs at two
banks. The criminal notices that one ATM has a surveillance
camera nearby while the other bank appears to lack such
technology. Which person do you think is more likely to be
robbed? Surely the criminal is likely to choose the target who

is away from a camera. One expert explains: "There are no data available on how many crimes have been aborted by criminals because of the cameras but most citizen groups and police believe that the cameras provide some deterrent effect."[8]

While data on the effectiveness of video surveillance may be less than conclusive, there is no doubt that Americans overwhelmingly support the use of such surveillance techniques. A 2007 poll by ABC News found that Americans approve of such measures by a 3-to-1 ratio. In fact, the poll found that "majority support for surveillance cameras crosses political, ideological, and population groups."[9] The poll found that 71 percent supported cameras while only 25 percent opposed them.

Increased government surveillance is necessary in an age of global terrorism.

As this chapter's opening paragraph on 9/11 suggests, greater surveillance is necessary in an age of global terrorism. Congress

FROM THE BENCH

United States v. Torres, 751 F.2d 875, 883 (7th Cir. 1984)

We do not think the Fourth Amendment prevents the government from coping with the menace of this organization by installing and operating secret television cameras in the organization's safe houses. The benefits to the public safety are great, and the costs to personal privacy are modest. A safe house is not a home. No one lives in these apartments, amidst the bombs and other paraphernalia of terrorism. They are places dedicated exclusively to illicit business; and though the Fourth Amendment protects business premises as well as homes, the invasion of privacy caused by secretly televising the interior of business premises is less than that caused by secretly televising the interior of a home, while the social benefit of the invasion is greater when the organization under investigation runs a bomb factory than it would be if it ran a chop shop or a numbers parlor. There is no right to be let alone while assembling bombs in safe houses.

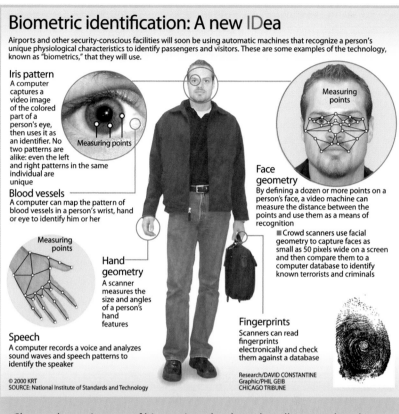

Biometric identification: A new IDea

Airports and other security-conscious facilities will soon be using automatic machines that recognize a person's unique physiological characteristics to identify passengers and visitors. These are some examples of the technology, known as "biometrics," that they will use.

Iris pattern
A computer captures a video image of the colored part of a person's eye, then uses it as an identifier. No two patterns are alike: even the left and right patterns in the same individual are unique

Measuring points

Measuring points

Face geometry
By defining a dozen or more points on a person's face, a video machine can measure the distance between the points and use them as a means of recognition

■ Crowd scanners use facial geometry to capture faces as small as 50 pixels wide on a screen and then compare them to a computer database to identify known terrorists and criminals

Blood vessels
A computer can map the pattern of blood vessels in a person's wrist, hand or eye to identify him or her

Measuring points

Hand geometry
A scanner measures the size and angles of a person's hand features

Fingerprints
Scanners can read fingerprints electronically and check them against a database

Speech
A computer records a voice and analyzes sound waves and speech patterns to identify the speaker

© 2000 KRT
SOURCE: National Institute of Standards and Technology

Research/DAVID CONSTANTINE
Graphic/PHIL GEIB
CHICAGO TRIBUNE

Shown above, six types of biometric technology that allow people to be identified by their physical characteristics. Airports are using biometric technology to increase their security.

was correct to amend the Foreign Intelligence Surveillance Act (FISA) to deal with this terrifying threat. Certainly Congress should not weaken governmental powers under FISA, which has been a success for the law enforcement community. As James A. Baker said to the Senate Judiciary Committee in September 2007: "FISA collection has been extremely productive over the years. . . . Suffice it to say that the record will show that the original FISA contributed significantly to our successes against al Qaeda and other terrorist groups post 9/11, and that FISA worked during wartime."[10]

QUOTABLE

President George W. Bush Expressing Support for the FISA Amendments Act of 2008

Almost seven years have passed since that September morning when nearly 3,000 men, women, and children were murdered in our midst. The attack changed our country forever. We realized America was a nation at war against a ruthless and persistent enemy. We realized that these violent extremists would spare no effort to kill again. And in the aftermath of 9/11, few would have imagined that we would be standing here seven years later without another attack on American soil.

The fact that the terrorists have failed to strike our shores again does not mean that our enemies have given up. To the contrary, since 9/11 they've plotted a number of attacks on our homeland. . . . One of the important lessons learned after 9/11 was that America's intelligence professionals lacked some of the tools they needed to monitor the communications of terrorists abroad. It is essential that our intelligence community know who our enemies are talking to, what they're saying, and what they're planning. Last year Congress passed temporary legislation that helped our intelligence community monitor these communications.

The legislation I am signing today will ensure that our intelligence community professionals have the tools they need to protect our country in the years to come. The DNI [Director of National Intelligence] and the Attorney General both report that, once enacted, this law will provide vital assistance to our intelligence officials in their work to thwart terrorist plots. This law will ensure that those companies whose assistance is necessary to protect the country will themselves be protected from lawsuits from past or future cooperation with the government. This law will protect the liberties of our citizens while maintaining the vital flow of intelligence. This law will play a critical role in helping to prevent another attack on our soil.

Source: Remarks of President George W. Bush upon signing FISA Amendments Act, H.R. 6304. http://www.usdoj.gov/archive/ll/docs/fisa-amendments-act-2008.pdf.

Richard Posner explains that "FISA in its pre-amendment form remains usable for regulating the monitoring of communications of known terrorists, but it is useless for finding out who is a terrorist."[11] Critics charge that increasing the government's power under FISA to conduct surveillance will lead to many innocent people being caught in the crosshairs—something Posner refers to as "false positives." He points out, however, that concern over false positives must be balanced against the greater danger of a false negative. "The failure to detect the 9/11 plot was an exceptionally costly false negative," he writes. "The intelligence services have no alternative to casting a wide net with a fine mesh if they are to have reasonable prospects of obtaining the clues that will enable future terrorist attacks on the United States to be prevented."[12]

In order to address some of these concerns, Congress passed the FISA Amendments Act in July 2008.[13] This law offers the government needed tools to combat the evils of terrorism, including a provision giving immunity from lawsuits to those private companies that help the government in tracking down suspected terrorist communications. Although many associate the FISA Amendments Act with the George W. Bush administration, then-Senator Barack Obama voted *for* this legislation, because he, like President Bush, recognized that the country was still in danger. Surveillance powers under FISA are not evil; they are necessary to ensure the security of the United States.

Summary

Nearly everyone agrees that some degree of surveillance is needed to ensure a basic level of security. Surveillance helps to deter crime and terrorism. Common sense tells you that if people believe they are being watched or monitored, they are less likely to engage in wrongdoing. Surveillance cameras have had notable successes in ensuring safety in housing projects, on city buses, and on public streets, and in even curtailing traffic violations. On a broader scale, surveillance is a resource our intelligence community can use to prevent another terrorist attack on American soil. That may represent the strongest argument in favor of surveillance—the prevention of another 9/11.

Increasingly Intrusive Newsgathering Efforts Threaten Privacy Rights

The press is overstepping in every direction the obvious bounds of propriety and of decency. Gossip is no longer the resource of the idle and of the vicious, but has become a trade, which is pursued with industry as well as effrontery.[1]

You might think—given the prevalence of modern-day tabloid newspapers and intrusive paparazzi—that the above-quoted statement was uttered in the late twentieth or early twenty-first century. This statement about the penchant of the press to invade the privacy of others, however, came from the pens of Boston-based lawyers Louis Brandeis (the future U.S. Supreme Court justice) and Samuel Warren in 1890.

Writing in the *Harvard Law Review*, the two partners and former law school classmates at Harvard argued that privacy laws

45

should evolve to protect people's "right to be let alone."[2] Legend has it that Warren became interested in exploring the idea of protecting privacy rights after a Boston newspaper reported on Warren's wife and daughter at high-society parties. While others have debunked this claim as myth, the reality is that many people in the late nineteenth century believed the press was going too far in reporting on people's private lives. One can only imagine what they would think of our modern media.[3]

With remarkable foresight, Warren and Brandeis saw that improved technological capabilities increased the press's access to the private lives of individuals. "Instantaneous photographs and newspaper enterprise have invaded the sacred precincts of private and domestic life," wrote the two law partners, "and numerous mechanical devices threaten to make good the prediction that what is whispered in the closet shall be proclaimed from the house-tops."[4] Fast-forward more than 100 years and it is clear that two of the major threats to privacy in our time come from the conduct of the media and advancement of technology.

Courts have recognized that some newsgathering techniques are often too intrusive.

No one denies that the media must gather news in order to report on important issues to the public. The problem lies in how they do it. The press cannot engage in unlawful behavior simply because its ultimate goal is legitimate and beneficial to society. The courts have ruled that certain unsavory practices by the news media are unjustified. Some courts have determined that newsgathering techniques have violated the branch of tort-law privacy known as intrusion upon seclusion, or simply intrusion. The *Restatement (Second) of Torts* —a highly valued source of law—describes an intruder as "one who intentionally intrudes, physically or otherwise, upon the solitude or seclusion of another or his private affairs or concerns."[5]

Perhaps the most well known example of intrusive conduct by members of the media occurred in France in 1997, when a group of paparazzi chased a black Mercedes traveling at excessive speeds down a highway. The Mercedes crashed, killing three people, including one of the most famous people in the world: Diana, Princess of Wales—the mother of the future king of England. French authorities detained seven paparazzi and considered filing criminal charges against them for their possible role in the accident.[6] Several of the paparazzi, in fact, took pictures of Diana and her driver as they lay in the crashed vehicle. Although charges were pursued, a French court dropped manslaughter charges against several of the paparazzi. The tragedy, however, led to repeated calls for anti-paparazzi legislation in the United States that would prevent intrusive conduct even in the pursuit of news.[7] Despite the crash and calls for legislation to prevent similar incidents, years after the Diana debacle, paparazzi still engage in reckless behavior in pursuit of celebrity images. There have been reports of would-be photographers intentionally running into cars carrying celebrities to have a chance to shoot high-priced photos.[8] Of this kind of aggressive pursuit, Oscar-winning actress Halle Berry said: "The last thing you want to sound like is a crybaby. I do understand the First Amendment and I understand the right of the paparazzi. I think the problem is they are crossing the line."[9] In other words, the paparazzi have become the "stalkerazzi."[10]

Tabloid journalists and annoying paparazzi are not the only ones who perpetrate these kinds of intrusions. Even employees of more traditional media outlets have engaged in the kind of intrusive behavior that crosses the line. For example, federal courts ruled in 1971 that *Life* reporters invaded the privacy of a man who practiced medicine without a license when they used false pretenses to obtain entrance to his house and then photographed him with a hidden camera. A.A. Dietemann practiced healing through the use of clay, minerals, and herbs. Two *Life* employees, pretending to know one of Dietemann's friends, sought his "medical" services. One of the undercover reporters then used a hidden camera to photograph Dietemann engaging in his practice, and secretly recorded the conversation. The photos later appeared in a *Life* story titled "Crackdown on Quackery."[11] The story later led to Dietemann facing charges of practicing medicine without a license. A federal District Court and later a federal appeals court in *Dietemann v. Time* agreed that the reporters had invaded Dietemann's privacy.

The Ninth U.S. Circuit Court of Appeals wrote that "we have little difficulty in concluding that clandestine photography of the plaintiff in his den and the recordation and transmission of his conversation without his consent resulting in his emotional distress warrants recovery for invasion of privacy in California."[12] The news reporters argued that the First Amendment shielded them from liability, but the federal appeals court rejected that claim, writing that "The First Amendment is not a license to

FROM THE BENCH

Dietemann v. Time, 449 F.2d 245, 249–250 (9ᵗʰ Cir. 1971)

The defendant claims that the First Amendment immunizes it from liability for invading plaintiff's den with a hidden camera and its concealed electronic instruments because its employees were gathering news and its instrumentalities are indispensable tools of investigative reporting. We agree that newsgathering is an integral part of news dissemination. We strongly disagree, however, that the hidden mechanical contrivances are indispensable tools of newsgathering. Investigative reporting is an ancient art; its successful practice long antecedes the invention of miniature cameras and electronic devices. The First Amendment has never been construed to accord newsmen immunity from torts or crimes committed during the course of newsgathering. The First Amendment is not a license to trespass, to steal, or to intrude by electronic means into the precincts of another's home or office. It does not become such a license simply because the person subjected to the intrusion is reasonably suspected of committing a crime....

Indeed, the Court strongly indicates that there is no First Amendment interest in protecting news media from calculated misdeeds.

trespass, to steal, or to intrude by electronic means into the precincts of another's home or office."[13]

Paparazzo Ron Galella virtually stalked the widow of former President John F. Kennedy, Jacqueline Kennedy Onassis, and her young children, John Jr. and Caroline, in his quest to take commercially profitable pictures. On one occasion, Galella jumped into the path of young John Kennedy while the boy was riding his bicycle. Another time he interrupted young Caroline Kennedy while she was playing tennis. He drove a powerboat within a few feet of Mrs. Onassis while she was swimming. He even bribed doormen at restaurants and romanced a Kennedy family servant to discover the family's movements.[14] Such intrusive conduct led a trial court judge to issue an injunction prohibiting Galella from coming within a certain distance of the former first lady and her family. Galella asserted that the First Amendment protected him from sanction for his newsgathering activities. The federal court rejected that argument, noting that "there is no threat to a free press in requiring its agents to act within the law."[15]

Another example of intrusive newsgathering conduct involved a planned exposé on the television program *Inside Edition*, which would have revealed the salaries of top executives at a major health care company, U.S. Healthcare. When the chairman of the board of the company declined to grant an interview to *Inside Edition*, reporters with the program began a pattern of intense surveillance of the daughter and son-in-law of the chairman, who themselves were high-ranking employees with the company. The "newsgathering" conduct consisted of the following the family members in their cars and parking outside their home on public streets. A federal District Court in Pennsylvania ruled in *Wolfson v. Lewis* (1996) that the intense surveillance amounted to unlawful intrusion: "Conduct that amounts to a persistent course of hounding, harassment, and unreasonable surveillance, even if conducted in a public or semi-public place, may nevertheless rise to the level of invasion of

FROM THE BENCH

Galella v. Onassis, 487 F.2d 986, 992–995 (2nd Cir. 1973)

Some examples of Galella's conduct brought out at trial are illustrative. Galella took pictures of John Kennedy [Jr.] riding his bicycle in Central Park across the way from his home. He jumped out into the boy's path, causing the agents concern for John's safety. The agents' reaction and interrogation of Galella led to Galella's arrest and his action against the agents; Galella on other occasions interrupted Caroline at tennis, and invaded the children's private schools. At one time he came uncomfortably close in a power boat to Mrs. Onassis swimming. He often jumped and postured around while taking pictures of her party, notably at a theater opening but also on numerous other occasions. He followed a practice of bribing apartment house, restaurant and nightclub doormen as well as romancing a family servant to keep him advised of the movements of the family....

Discrediting all of Galella's testimony the court found the photographer guilty of harassment, intentional infliction of emotional distress, assault and battery, commercial exploitation of defendant's personality, and invasion of privacy. Fully crediting defendant's testimony, the court found no liability on Galella's claim. Evidence offered by the defense showed that Galella had on occasion intentionally physically touched Mrs. Onassis and her daughter, caused fear of physical contact in his frenzied attempts to get their pictures, followed defendant and her children too closely in an automobile, endangered the safety of the children while they were swimming, water skiing and horseback riding. Galella cannot successfully challenge the court's finding of tortuous conduct....

Of course legitimate countervailing social needs may warrant some intrusion despite an individual's reasonable expectation of privacy and freedom from harassment. However the interference allowed may be no greater than that necessary to protect the overriding public interest. Mrs. Onassis was properly found to be a public figure and thus subject to news coverage.... Nonetheless, Galella's action went far beyond the reasonable bounds of news gathering. When weighed against the *de minimis* public importance of the daily activities of the defendant, Galella's constant surveillance, his obtrusive and intruding presence, was unwarranted and unreasonable. If there were any doubt in our minds, Galella's inexcusable conduct toward defendant's minor children would resolve it.

The pioneering paparazzo Ron Galella following former first lady Jacqueline Kennedy Onassis on the streets of New York City, circa 1971. As a result of a lawsuit filed by Onassis, he was restricted from coming within 100 yards of her home and within 50 yards of her or her children, Caroline and John Jr.

privacy based intrusion upon seclusion."[16] The court concluded that "a course of repeated harassment that amounts to hounding and becomes a substantial burden to a person may constitute an invasion of privacy."[17]

Privacy must be expanded to cover technological advancements.

In 1890, Brandeis and Warren warned of "numerous mechanical devices" that threaten privacy ever more. In an age populated by cell phone cameras and other powerful technological advances, privacy laws and privacy rulings must expand to protect individuals' rights to be let alone. The state of California, which is home to a large number of celebrities and paparazzi, responded to this problem by amending its privacy law to protect against "constructive invasions of privacy."[18] The California law provides:

> A person is liable for constructive invasion of privacy when the defendant attempts to capture, in a manner that is offensive to a reasonable person, any type of visual image, sound recording, or other physical impression of the plaintiff engaging in a personal or familial activity under circumstances in which the plaintiff had a reasonable expectation of privacy, through the use of a visual or auditory enhancing device, regardless of whether there is a physical trespass, if this image, sound recording, or other physical impression could not have been achieved without a trespass unless the visual or auditory enhancing device was used.[19]

This law has become necessary in today's world where technology can capture private conversations 50 feet away. The widespread use of camera phones has caused invasions of privacy to multiply. The use by some unscrupulous individuals of camera phones has led to a new criminal term called upskirting, in which an individual shoots photos of women up their dresses.[20] Many states have laws, often called video voyeurism laws, that are designed to criminalize this type of behavior. Some courts, however, have ruled that such laws do not apply in public places where people can have no reasonable expectation of privacy. For example, the Supreme Court of Washington ruled in *State v. Glas* (2002) that the statute did not apply to a criminal defendant who took such pictures of women in a shopping mall. The Court wrote that "public places could not logically constitute locations where a person could reasonably expect to be safe from casual or hostile intrusion or surveillance."[21] The Court added that "other state courts have faced similar frustration when confronted with acts of voyeurism, but with no statute clearly covering the challenged violations."[22] For this reason, many legal scholars have called for legislators and the courts to respond flexibly by recognizing a right to privacy even in public places.[23] The rights granted under the U.S. Constitution protect people, not places.

Summary

People deserve to live in a society that respects their privacy rights. The right to be let alone is, as Justice Louis Brandeis wrote in 1928, "the most comprehensive of rights and the right most valued by civilized men."[24] The modern media often invade individuals' privacy in the pursuit of their newsgathering function. There is no First Amendment defense to intrusive, harassing conduct, even if it leads to the publication of truthful, important information. It is not just the paparazzi but also other members of the media who violate this principle.

The protection of privacy becomes even more important as technological capabilities increase and invasions of privacy become more intense and frequent. In the age of cell phone cameras, telescopic lenses, upskirting, and digital infringements on privacy online, the need for privacy protection continues to increase.

The Constitution Protects Even Aggressive Newsgathering

About a century ago, an enterprising journalist named Upton Sinclair went undercover to discover whether there was any truth to disturbing rumors about the unsanitary conditions in the Chicago meatpacking industry. What he found was appalling—rat-infested food, meat with mold, and other abominable and unsanitary conditions that threatened the nation's food supply. He recorded his findings in *The Jungle*, a novel that contributed to the ultimate passage of the Food and Drug Act of 1906.[1] In a similar piece of investigative journalism from a decade prior to Sinclair's work, newspaper reporter Nellie Bly pretended to have a mental illness in order to gain access to a women's insane asylum in New York City. Bly then wrote in the *New York World* about the mistreatment and abuse she witnessed. This led to a grand jury investigation and, later, reform of the industry.[2] In a more recent example, Jerry Thompson, a reporter for a Nashville,

54

The American journalist and author Nellie Bly (1864-1922) became famous for an undercover exposé in which she faked insanity to reveal the widespread abuses occurring in mental institutions. Bly's reporting is an example of the kind of aggressive newsgathering that receives constitutional protection because of its benefits to society.

Tennessee-based newspaper, infiltrated the Ku Klux Klan and related his experiences in his 1982 book, *My Life in the Klan*.[3] These are but some examples of the kinds of important public revelations that have been achieved through surreptitious conduct by members of the media.

The importance of the information should help provide broad protection for newsgathering.

No less an authority than the U.S. Supreme Court recognized that "without some protection for seeking out the news, freedom of the press could be eviscerated."[4] The problem is that the Supreme Court has provided too little protection for newsgathering, particularly as compared with publication. In other words, even though newsgathering and publication go hand in hand, the courts often label newsgathering as unprotected conduct and publication as protected speech. This ignores the practical reality that it is only through the newsgathering efforts, which are sometimes intrusive, that publication of important information can occur.

Legal scholar Erwin Chemerinsky argues that "there is a need for First Amendment safeguards for undercover media operations that serve an important public purpose."[5] He explains: "The very notion of a marketplace of ideas rests on the availability of information. Aggressive newsgathering, such as by undercover reporters, is often the key to gathering the information. People on their own cannot expose unhealthy practices in supermarkets or fraud by telemarketers or unnecessary surgery by doctors. But, the media can expose this, if it is allowed the tools to do so, and the public directly benefits from the reporting."[6] Professor C. Thomas Dienes echoes these sentiments by pointing out that "undercover journalism often serves the public interest" and that "it allows the media to perform its role as the eyes and ears of the people, to perform a checking function on government."[7]

John Wade, a pioneer scholar in the area of tort law, contended years ago that the "nature of the information that he [an investigative reporter] was seeking to obtain" should factor into courts' analysis as to whether the newsgathering should receive constitutional protection.[8]

Better-reasoned court decisions limit the privacy and other tort claims against those who engage in newsgathering for an important purpose.

Some court decisions have recognized the importance of the information published from the newsgathering process and have eliminated or limited liability accordingly. In *Desnick v. American Broadcasting Co.* (1995), the Seventh U.S. Circuit Court of Appeals rejected a variety of tort claims, including state privacy law claims, against a broadcast entity for sending false patients into an eye clinic to see whether the doctors and staff would recommend unnecessary eye treatments to make money.[9] The Seventh Circuit emphasized the importance of the information and the fact that the story was true. It diminished—and ultimately rejected—the tort claims of the plaintiff in the case.

The *Desnick* court drew an analogy to "testers" used by those investigating or exploring housing discrimination claims under the Fair Housing Act. Sometimes civil rights commissions may employ persons to pose as prospective buyers or sellers to "test" whether a landlord will discriminate against them based on race, familial status, or some other protected characteristic. Even though the "testers" engage in a form of deceptive conduct by pretending to be somebody else, they are not considered to be violating privacy interests. In one testing case, a court acknowledged the deceit but said it was immaterial: "This element of deceit has no significant effect here. Courts have consistently upheld the otherwise legal use of informants in criminal proceedings."[10]

Like defamation law, privacy law needs to be tempered.

The First Amendment receives a healthy degree of respect in defamation law. Defamation—the term used for both libel and slander—refers to a false statement that harms someone's reputation. For example, if a person claims that I, the author of this book, am a convicted sex offender, this would be a patently false statement that would not only harm this author's reputation, but would also give me basis for a claim for defamation.

Defamation law does not impose automatic liability for all mistakes of fact. Defamation law, particularly defamation claims

FROM THE BENCH

Desnick v. American Broadcasting Co., 44 F.3d 1345, 1353, 1355 (7th Cir. 1995)

No embarrassingly intimate details of anybody's life were publicized in the present case. There was no eavesdropping on a private conversation; the testers recorded their own conversations with the Desnick Eye Center's physicians. There was no violation of the doctor-patient privilege. There was no theft [of], or intent to steal, trade secrets; no disruption of decorum, of peace and quiet; no noisy or distracting demonstrations. Had the testers been undercover FBI agents, there would have been no violation of the Fourth Amendment, because there would have been no invasion of a legally protected interest in property or privacy. ... "Testers" who pose as prospective home buyers in order to gather evidence of housing discrimination are not trespassers even if they are private persons not acting under color of law. The situation of the defendants' "testers" is analogous. Like testers seeking evidence of violation of antidiscrimination laws, the defendants' test patients gained entry into the plaintiffs' premises by misrepresenting their purposes (more precisely by a misleading omission to disclose those purposes). But the entry was not invasive in the sense of infringing the kind of interest of the plaintiffs that the law of trespass protects; it was not an interference with the ownership or possession of land. ...

What we have said largely disposes of two other claims—infringement of the right of privacy, and illegal wiretapping. The right of privacy embraces several filed by public officials on matters of public interest, must be assuaged by what the U.S. Supreme Court called "profound national commitment to the principle that debate on public issues should be uninhibited, robust, and wide-open, and that it may well include vehement, caustic, and sometimes unpleasantly sharp attacks on government and public officials."[11] The high court explained that not even some false statements could constitute defamation because they would chill First Amendment-protected activities and prevent the media from reporting on controversial issues. Thus, the Court fashioned a rule that provided that public officials who sue for defamation

distinct interests, but the only ones conceivably involved here are the closely related interests in concealing intimate personal facts and in preventing intrusion into legitimately private activities, such as phone conversations....

One further point about the claims concerning the making of the program segment, as distinct from the content of the segment itself, needs to be made. The Supreme Court in the name of the First Amendment has hedged about defamation suits, even when not brought by public figures, with many safeguards designed to protect a vigorous market in ideas and opinions. Today's "tabloid" style investigative television reportage, conducted by networks desperate for viewers in an increasingly competitive television market,... constitutes—although it is often shrill, one-sided, and offensive, and sometimes defamatory—an important part of that market. It is entitled to all the safeguards with which the Supreme Court has surrounded liability for defamation. And it is entitled to them regardless of the name of the tort,... and, we add, regardless of whether the tort suit is aimed at the content of the broadcast or the production of the broadcast. If the broadcast itself does not contain actionable defamation, and no established rights are invaded in the process of creating it (for the media have no general immunity from tort or contract liability), then the target has no legal remedy even if the investigatory tactics used by the network are surreptitious, confrontational, unscrupulous, and ungentlemanly.

must show by "convincing clarity" that the alleged defamer acted with "actual malice"—defined as knowing a statement was false or acting in "reckless disregard" as to whether the statement was true or false.[12]

"A rule compelling the critic of official conduct to guarantee the truth of all his factual assertions—and to do so on pain of libel judgments virtually unlimited in amount—leads to a comparable 'self-censorship,'" the Supreme Court explained in its decision.[13] In other words, the highest court in the country changed defamation law by making sure that the First Amendment played a crucial role in its development. The courts need to follow the same path and recognize, as professor Paul LeBel persuasively argues, "the constitutional significance" of newsgathering.[14] He suggests the following rule: "Courts should balance the state interest that is served by the legal rule sought to be applied against the representative of the press arising out of the newsgathering activity against the First Amendment interest that is served by the acquisition of the information through that activity."[15]

QUOTABLE

Professor Paul LeBel, legal commentator

One of the lessons that emerges most clearly from the defamation and privacy arena is that an individual can be classified as a public figure and thereby be deprived of some measure of common law tort protection against defamation and invasion of privacy. This occurs because of a legitimate public interest in the publication of information about some aspect of the public figure's life. Against that constitutional background, no great leap of imagination is required to envision an analogous category of information that is in the public interest, albeit not yet in the public domain.

Source: Paul A. LeBel, "The Constitutional Interest in Getting the News: Toward a First Amendment Protection from Tort Liability for Surreptitious Newsgathering," 4 *William & Mary Bill of Rights Journal* 1145, 1152-1153 (1996).

This doesn't mean that the press should be given a free pass to do whatever it wants in pursuit of a story. Obviously, no reporter, for example, should be given constitutional protection for committing a murder or a serious assault in order to obtain important information. Both the First Amendment and the public's interest in the ultimate information, however, should be factored into the equation. LeBel says that "the First Amendment protection for acquisition of information can be overcome by a stronger state interest in forbidding certain activity and in attaching criminal and civil sanctions to conduct that contravenes those prohibitions."[16]

The problem is that unless newsgathering is given a healthy degree of First Amendment protection, there will be a drastic limitation on the ability of investigative reporters to ferret out and report on important stories. Attorney Kathleen Kirby argues that "we should fight for a vigorous press that is free to conduct responsible investigations of newsworthy stories with a constitutional shield of some meaningful dimension."[17]

Summary

Members of the media have brought countless important stories to the public's attention because they were willing to delve deeply into their investigations and engage in intrusive newsgathering activities. That work has led to the publication of important information—such as unsanitary food-handling practices, the abuse of the mentally ill, government corruption, and other issues of public concern. The odd disconnect about the state of the law is that *publication* receives a high degree of First Amendment protection, while the *newsgathering* that directly led to the publication receives very little. That situation must be rectified.

Employees Need and Deserve Greater Privacy Protections in the Workplace

You log on to your computer at work when you arrive a few minutes early. You browse the Internet, check your Facebook page, send a couple of e-mails to family and friends, and make one personal call from your employer's phone. Then, you start your workday, diligently performing the job-related tasks that you have been asked to do. Occasionally, you might respond to a personal e-mail and make a personal telephone call.

Later that week you receive a memorandum from human resources that warns you about using your computer, phone, and e-mail system for personal use. The memorandum also warns you about going to inappropriate Web sites and reminds you that employees are supposed to use the Internet for business purposes only. Your supervisor questions whether you have enough work to do. You soon realize that Big Brother of *1984* is on the job in your workplace. Rest assured you are not alone.

Recent studies show that many employers routinely monitor their employees' e-mail usage. Some retain and review employee e-mails. Others install monitoring software that enables them to review what keystrokes an employee enters into his or her computer. They track the sites you visit and the phone calls you make. A 2005 survey by the American Management Association and The ePolicy Institute found that 55 percent of employers reviewed employee e-mail and 36 percent tracked content and keystrokes entered by employees on their computers.[1] "The snooping often includes all activity over the company's network

FROM THE BENCH

O'Connor v. Ortega, 480 U.S. 709, 716-718 (1987)

Within the workplace context, this Court has recognized that employees may have a reasonable expectation of privacy against intrusions by police.... As with the expectation of privacy in one's home, such an expectation in one's place of work is based upon societal expectations that have deep roots in the history of the [Fourth] Amendment....

Given the societal expectations of privacy in one's place of work ... we reject the contention made by the Solicitor General and petitioners that public employees can never have a reasonable expectation of privacy in their place of work. Individuals do not lose Fourth Amendment rights merely because they work for the government instead of a private employer.... The employee's expectation of privacy must be assessed in the context of the employment relation.... Given the great variety of work environments in the public sector, the question whether an employee has a reasonable expectation of privacy must be addressed on a case-by-case basis.

The Court of Appeals concluded that Dr. Ortega had a reasonable expectation of privacy in his office and five Members of this Court agree with that determination.... we recognize that the undisputed evidence suggests that Dr. Ortega had a reasonable expectation of privacy in his desk and file cabinets. The undisputed evidence discloses that Dr. Ortega did not share his desk or file cabinets with any other employees.

and allows bosses to read a worker's comments when blogging, instant messaging and participating in online chat rooms."[2]

Excessive employee monitoring and surveillance has negative ramifications.

Monitoring of employees via electronic surveillance can have many negative effects on employees. Professors Joseph Migga Kizza and Jackline Ssanyu in their article "Workplace Surveillance" identify numerous such effects, including a lack of trust among workers and management, stress, repetitive strain disorders, loss of individual creativity, reduced peer support, loss of self-esteem, worker alienation, a loss of communication, and other psychological effects.[3]

They explain that "employee monitoring has the potential to undermine workplace morale and create distrust and suspicion between employees and their supervisors or management."[4] In turn, the reduced morale can lead to an increase in official complaints, privacy lawsuits, and other turmoil in the workplace. Perhaps the most obvious downside of employee monitoring concerns stress, as the constant surveillance can cause employees to feel nervous and anxious on the job, which may lead to decreased job performance and increased sicknesses. A more underrated cause of such surveillance is the loss of self-esteem. "The isolation, monotony of work, and lack of freedom to vary job steps lower employee morale and consequently self-esteem."[5]

Researcher David Zweig explains that surveillance does have a negative psychological effect in the workplace. His years of research indicate that employee monitoring "continues to violate the basic psychological boundaries between the employer and the employee—one that is predicated on some minimal level of privacy, autonomy, and respect."[6] He also reports another negative effect of excessive employee monitoring, a high rate of turnover: "In fact, alarmingly high levels of turnover have been reported among monitored employees in some organizations."[7]

Employees do not lose all expectations of privacy at work.

The Fourth Amendment and its proscription against "unreasonable searches and seizures" can provide constitutional protection against certain invasive actions by public employers. For example, in *O'Connor v. Ortega* (1987), the Supreme Court determined that government employees do have, depending upon the particular facts and situation, reasonable expectations of privacy in their workplace. "Individuals do not lose Fourth Amendment

FROM THE BENCH

Avila v. Valentin-Maldonado, No. 06-1285, (D. PR) (2008)

Defendants base their need for conducting covert surveillance in this case on their interest in eradicating sexual harassment and discrimination in the employment setting. Further, they argue that previous steps to correct the problem had proven ineffective in correcting the situation.

It is axiomatic that sexual harassment and discrimination negatively affect the working environment. However, apart from the fact that the documents submitted in this case pertain just to one particular alleged victim—as opposed to the "rash of complaints by female police officers" referred to by defendants—there is no evidence in the record indicative that any of the alleged sexual discriminatory conduct took place in the locker-break room. In other words, there does not seem to be a logical connection between the conduct sought to be curtailed and the preventive measures taken. All we have before us is reference to the two anonymous notes whose content in no way manifest an impending danger situation.

Accordingly, faced with the limited information currently available to the court it cannot be reasonably concluded that defendants had a valid reason to have covert cameras installed in the locker-break room. In other words, even though defendants have a legitimate interest in eradicating sexual discrimination in the workplace there is not sufficient evidence in the record at this time to warrant encroachment into plaintiffs' privacy interests via surveillance video.

rights merely because they work for the government instead of a private employer," the Court wrote.[8]

Some courts have determined that public employers violate the Fourth Amendment when they surreptitiously record

FROM THE BENCH

Quon v. Arch Wireless Operating Co., 529 F.3d 892, 904-906 (9th Cir. 2008)

The extent to which the Fourth Amendment provides protection for the contents of electronic communications in the Internet age is an open question. The recently minted standard of electronic communication via e-mails, text messages, and other means opens a new frontier in Fourth Amendment jurisprudence that has been little explored. Here, we must first answer the threshold question: Do users of text messaging services such as those provided by Arch Wireless have a reasonable expectation of privacy in their text messages stored on the service provider's network? We hold that they do.

In *Katz v. United States* (1967), the government placed an electronic listening device on a public telephone booth, which allowed the government to listen to the telephone user's conversation. ... The Supreme Court held that listening to the conversation through the electronic device violated the user's reasonable expectation of privacy. In so holding, the Court reasoned, "One who occupies [a phone booth], shuts the door behind him, and pays the toll that permits him to place a call is surely entitled to assume that the words he utters into the mouthpiece will not be broadcast to the world. To read the Constitution more narrowly is to ignore the vital role that the public telephone has come to play in private communication." Therefore, "[t]he Government's activities in electronically listening to and recording the petitioner's words violated the privacy upon which he justifiably relied while using the telephone booth and thus constituted a 'search and seizure' within the meaning of the Fourth Amendment."

On the other hand, the Court has also held that the government's use of a pen register—a device that records the phone numbers one dials—does not violate the Fourth Amendment. This is because people "realize that they must 'convey' phone numbers to the telephone company, since it is through telephone company switching equipment that their calls are completed." The Court distinguished *Katz* by noting that "a pen register differs significantly from the listening device employed in *Katz*, for pen registers do not acquire the *contents* of communications."

and watch the activities of employees in certain areas of the workplace generally outside of public view. Consider *Avila v. Valentin-Maldonado*, the case of 22 police officers who filed a lawsuit after their employer conducted secret video surveillance

This distinction also applies to written communications, such as letters. It is well-settled that, "since 1878, ... the Fourth Amendment's protection against 'unreasonable searches and seizures' protects a citizen against the warrantless opening of sealed letters and packages addressed to him in order to examine the contents." ...

Our Internet jurisprudence is instructive. In *United States v. Forrester*, we held that "e-mail ... users have no expectation of privacy in the to/from addresses of their messages ... because they should know that this information is provided to and used by Internet service providers for the specific purpose of directing the routing of information." ... Thus, we have extended the pen register and outside-of-envelope rationales to the "to/from" line of e-mails. But we have not ruled on whether persons have a reasonable expectation of privacy in the content of e-mails... we explicitly noted that "e-mail to/from addresses ... constitute addressing information and do not necessarily reveal any more about the underlying contents of communication than do phone numbers." ... Thus, we concluded that "[t]he privacy interests in these two forms of communication [letters and e-mails] are identical," and that, while "[t]he contents may deserve Fourth Amendment protection ... the address and size of the package do not."

We see no meaningful difference between the e-mails at issue in *Forrester* and the text messages at issue here. Both are sent from user to user via a service provider that stores the messages on its servers. Similarly, as in *Forrester*, we also see no meaningful distinction between text messages and letters. As with letters and e-mails, it is not reasonable to expect privacy in the information used to "address" a text message, such as the dialing of a phone number to send a message. However, users do have a reasonable expectation of privacy in the content of their text messages vis-à-vis the service provider.... That Arch Wireless may have been able to access the contents of the messages for its own purposes is irrelevant.... Appellants did not expect that Arch Wireless would monitor their text messages, much less turn over the messages to third parties without Appellants' consent.

of them in the locker room and break room. A reviewing federal District Court determined that the officers stated a valid claim under the Fourth Amendment. The court explained that "there is sufficient indicia in the record that the locker-break room was intended to be used by a limited group of people for activities intended to be carried out outside the presence of the general public to meet both the subjective and objective requirements under the Fourth Amendment. The purpose of the room was inherently private."[9]

More specifically to the question of electronic surveillance, a federal appeals court recently ruled that the city of Ontario, California, violated the privacy rights of a police officer when it read his personal text messages from his work pager. The city contracted with a company for its wireless services for its employees' pagers. The wireless company released the text messages of employees, even personal ones, to the city employer. Several employees sued the wireless company and the city for violations of a part of the Electronic Communications Act of 1986, also known as the Stored Communications Act, and for violating the employees' Fourth Amendment rights.

The Ninth U.S. Circuit Court of Appeals ruled in *Quon v. Arch Wireless Operating Co.* (2008) that the wireless company violated federal privacy law and that the city arguably violated the employees' Fourth Amendment rights.[10] The appeals court reasoned that employees who use text-messaging services do have a reasonable expectation of privacy in their text messages.

Summary

The monitoring of employees will only continue in the future, particularly as technological advancements continue to proliferate at a speedy rate. Given this development, the law should recognize that employees have a right to retain reasonable expectations of privacy in the workplace. If the legal system fails to accord workers sufficient privacy rights, not only will individual citizens' privacy be under threat, but the productivity of the workplace will suffer.

Employees care deeply about their privacy. Electronic monitoring not only causes stress, but also leads to worker alienation and can stifle creativity. Make no mistake about it, this is one of the major privacy issues of our time. Professor William R. Corbett notes that "the most high-profile workplace privacy issue of the day is electronic monitoring of employee communications and activities."[11] He also explains that "electronic monitoring is an area where technology has outstripped the law, leaving employees largely unprotected."[12]

An even greater danger in the future will be the growing extent to which employers invade their workers' privacy rights at home. Author Frederick Lane, in his book *The Naked Employee*, writes that "the most perturbing development is the growing erasure of any distinction between work and home."[13] To combat this, the legal system must respond and develop a consistent body of statutory and judicial law to provide sufficient protection to employees from invasive monitoring by employers.

Employees Have Limited Expectations of Privacy in the Workplace

I magine you are the owner of a company and you became aware that your competitors are doing better in the market than you are. You look at the monthly reports and discover that productivity in the office seems to be on the wane. At first glance, you don't know why. You talk to the office manager, who reports that there are no immediate disruptions and your employees don't take an unusually high level of sick days. Still, something is wrong.

You ask the office manager to dig a little deeper and discover the source of the problem. The manager installs a program that monitors employees' online activity. The manager has heard reports in the industry that some employees have been spending a great deal of time online for personal pleasure, not for work-related activities. The results are stunning. Some of your employees are regularly playing poker online; others are watching their favorite television shows. Even more disturbing, two employees have accessed pornographic Web sites on company time. The manager also monitors and examines employees' e-mail. You discover that one employee is passing along company trade secrets to a competitor while trying to obtain a job with that competitor.

This hypothetical is no aberration; it is a daily reality for employers who want to ensure that employees are productive and actually working for the company. Many employers must monitor employees to assess productivity, deter theft of company property, watch out for commercial espionage, prevent harassment, and—the most pervasive problem of all—limit employees' personal use of the Internet on company time. For these reasons, more and more employers are monitoring their employees' electronic activities. The 2007 Electronic & Surveillance Survey from the American Management Association and The ePolicy Institute reported that 66 percent of employers monitored employees' Internet connections.[1]

Monitoring is essential for employers.

Privacy protections are at their zenith in the home, where people have a reasonable expectation of privacy. In the workplace, however, employees enter into the property or "home" of the employer. Employers must have the ability to protect their businesses, including their computer networks. In addition to having their employees surfing the Internet, playing computer games, or engaging in other nonwork-related activity instead of doing their jobs, employers can face legal liability for employees' offensive e-mail communications as well as other inappropriate, even unlawful activities committed online. Employers have a strong interest in preventing these sorts of problems.

Employees, on the other hand, have limited expectations of privacy in the workplace. From a constitutional perspective, employees have little to no reasonable expectation of privacy in what they do in the areas in which they work. This means that employees charged with crimes can seldom mount an effective Fourth Amendment-based defense to criminal charges. Take the example of *United States v. Gonzalez,* which involved a hospital worker who had shipped to himself from Belgium more than 3,600 grams of Ecstasy, an illegal drug.[2] A FedEx worker noticed something suspicious about the package in a Brussels warehouse that was addressed to a doctor in a public hospital in Bellflower, California. The U.S. Drug Enforcement Administration (DEA) contacted the hospital in California and installed a security camera in the hospital mailroom. The camera showed Jesus Daria Gonzalez, a transportation orderly, high-fiving another man upon opening the package in the hospital mailroom. Clearly, the two drug dealers were thrilled about successfully shipping illegal drugs. To their dismay, however, federal officials had caught them red-handed. Gonzalez later sued the government by claiming an invasion of privacy in violation of his Fourth Amendment rights.

Both a federal District Court and a federal appeals court rejected his Fourth Amendment claims and concluded that he had no reasonable expectation of privacy in a public area of his workplace.

While the Constitution generally protects people from governmental intrusion, government employees, like employees of private companies, also have limited expectations of privacy even for conduct that transpires in their individual offices. In *United States v. Reilly,* a federal District Court in New York determined that a Department of Labor employee had no reasonable expectation of privacy in his cubicle even when he was accessing material on the Internet during off-work hours. The defendant, who was accessing Web sites with child pornography, contended that federal agents violated his Fourth Amendment rights. The court disagreed, noting that "the fact that employees may have kept some personal items in their cubicles does not give the defendant a legitimate expectation of privacy in the cubicle."[3]

The court also rejected the defendant's assertion that his Fourth Amendment rights were violated when a federal agent seized his personal diskette. The court determined that "the government's seizure of the diskette falls into the exception carved out to the Fourth Amendment of a warrant and probable cause

FROM THE BENCH

United States v. Gonzalez, 328 F.3d 543, 548 (9th Cir. 2003)

Gonzalez would have us adopt a theory of the Fourth Amendment akin to J.K. Rowling's Invisibility Cloak, to create at will a shield impenetrable to law enforcement view even in the most public places. However, the fabric of the Fourth Amendment does not stretch that far. He did not have an expectation of privacy in the public mailroom that society would accept as reasonable.

The fact that the surveillance was conducted by video camera does not alter our conclusion. To be sure, video surveillance is subject to higher scrutiny under the Fourth Amendment.... A person has a stronger claim to a reasonable expectation of privacy from video surveillance than against a manual search.... Thus, we have held that the Fourth Amendment forbids warrantless videotaping of a private office,... and hotel rooms....

However, "[v]ideo surveillance does not in itself violate a reasonable expectation of privacy." .... Indeed, "[v]ideotaping of suspects in public places, such as banks, does not violate the Fourth Amendment; the police may record what they normally may view with the naked eye." ... We have not defined the precise contours of Fourth Amendment protection in the video context. However, in this case, given the public nature of the mailroom in a community hospital where individuals—even DEA agents—strolled nearby without impediment during the transaction, we conclude the defendant had no objectively reasonable expectation of privacy that would preclude video surveillance of activities already visible to the public.

Perhaps, as Edgar Allan Poe put it in *The Purloined Letter*, the best way to conceal something is to employ "the comprehensive and sagacious expedient of not attempting to conceal it at all." By taking delivery of contraband in the public mailroom of a community hospital, the defendant might well have succeeded in concealing his criminal acts. However, even though the Fourth Amendment recognizes temporary zones of privacy that are protected from warrantless intrusion, the defendant was not entitled to its protection in this case.

for the 'special needs' of the government in the efficient opera-
tion of a government workplace."[4]

Employers must be able to monitor employees' e-mail and Internet activity.

Courts routinely have determined that employees have limited,
if any, expectations of privacy in the workplace with respect to
e-mail and the Internet. There is a very good reason for this:
The material is the employer's property. The employer owns the
computer and e-mail system. The employee is only using the
employer's property.

For example, many courts have rejected claims by employees and ex-employees to privacy in the content of their e-mails.
A prime example is the case of *Smyth v. The Pillsbury Company*.[5]
In this decision, an employee made unflattering comments
about the company to a supervisor. The company had assured
its employees that all e-mail communications would remain private. The employer at a later date, however, intercepted several
of the employee's e-mail messages and, based on those messages,
terminated his employment.

The federal court hearing the case determined that there
was no "reasonable expectation of privacy in e-mail communications voluntarily made by an employee to his supervisor over the
company e-mail system notwithstanding any assurances that such
communications would not be intercepted by management."[6] The
court distinguished the reading of employee e-mail from a forced
urinalysis or a personal property search. According to the court,
the employee "voluntarily communicated the alleged unprofessional comments over the company e-mail system."[7]

Employers must protect themselves from legal liability and other problems.

The American Management Association and The ePolicy Institute
report that there are many valid reasons why employers monitor

their employees. Employers have a strong interest in ensuring that employees are doing the job that they are paid to perform. As legal commentator Stephen J. Stine explains, "Even your most conscientious employees may find it hard to resist paying bills online at work, checking their personal e-mail accounts, shopping online, or engaging in personal investment or online trading activities. Those seemingly innocuous activities lead to decreased weekly or even daily productivity."[8]

Furthermore, employers can face great legal liability if employees use the Internet and e-mail to traffic in obscene, racy, and profane jokes or material. "Simply put, the Internet opens many avenues for employees to engage in offensive or detrimental conduct," Stine writes. "One of your employees may download crude or obscene jokes and forward them to coworkers using the office e-mail system. Or an employee may download sexually explicit pictures and use them as a screensaver on his computer monitor."[9] Nancy Flynn, executive director of The ePolicy Institute says:

FROM THE BENCH

Smyth v. The Pillsbury Company, 914 F. Supp. 97, 101 (E.D. Pa. 1996)

[E]ven if we found that an employee had a reasonable expectation of privacy in the contents of his e-mail communications over the company e-mail system, we do not find that a reasonable person would consider the defendant's interception of these communications to be a substantial and highly offensive invasion of [the employee's] privacy. Again, we note that by intercepting such communications, the company is not, as in the case of urinalysis or personal property searches, requiring the employee to disclose any personal information about himself or invading the employee's person or personal effects. Moreover, the company's interest in preventing inappropriate and unprofessional comments or even illegal activity over its e-mail system outweighs any privacy interest the employee may have in those comments.

Concern over litigation and the role electronic evidence plays in lawsuits and regulatory investigations has spurred more employers to monitor online activity. . . . To help control the risk of litigation, security breaches and other electronic disasters, employers should take advantage of monitoring and blocking technology to battle people problems—including the accidental and intentional misuse of computer systems and other electronic resources.[10]

Another risk for employers arises if a disgruntled employee uses the employer's communications system to air company problems in public or, even worse, to disclose employer trade secrets or other confidential information online. These are real dangers that can easily occur unless employers vigorously monitor their employees' online activities. Finally, some employees just have a problem controlling their use of the Internet for personal business. Many employees, for example, do their Christmas shopping online at work. The phenomenon of e-commerce has become "the greatest abuse of online activities."[11]

At other times, employees may watch major sporting events or other entertainment on their computer rather than perform their work. A prime example is that of "March Madness," the time of the year when the National Collegiate Athletic Association (NCAA) basketball tournament takes place. One management consultant company reports that employees watching college basketball games at work "could cost employers as much as $1.7 billion in wasted work time over the 16 business days of the tournament."[12]

For all these reasons, many employers have installed blocking software that limits employee access to specific Web sites or categories of Web sites. According to a recent survey by the American Management Association and The ePolicy Institute, 65 percent of companies use such software to block connections to certain Web sites. In the survey, 96 percent of companies expressed concern about sexual or pornographic Web sites, 61 percent focused on limiting employee access to game sites, 50 percent said they were trying to limit access to social-networking sites, 27 percent were focused on shopping sites, and 21 percent focused on limiting employee access to sports sites.[13]

Summary

Employees are paid to perform work on company time. They are not paid to surf the Internet for personal pleasure, to chat on social-networking sites with friends and acquaintances, to engage in personal e-commerce, to watch sporting events online, or to access otherwise inappropriate material. Unfortunately, we live in an age of what has been termed "cyberslacking."[14] Employers have a right to combat this growing problem.

The Future
of Privacy Rights

Privacy is the battleground of the future.
　　　　　—Lee Levine, leading First Amendment attorney

A s the arguments in this book have demonstrated, privacy is a multi-layered concept that transcends many areas of the law. Privacy also continues to evolve, as newer forms of technology allow greater invasions and protections of privacy at the same time. Various aspects of privacy can cause controversy. This book examined three of those areas in some detail, but there are many others, such as behavioral targeting, cloud computing, digital-rights management, and genetic privacy.[1]

　　Some other important privacy issues concern whether the First Amendment should prohibit the government from limiting the flow of commercial information. Privacy advocates contend that allowing the government and private corporations

THE LETTER OF THE LAW

Data Privacy Resolution in the U.S. House of Representatives

H. Res. 31, January 2009

Whereas the Internet and the capabilities of modern technology cause data privacy issues to figure prominently in the lives of many people in the United States at work, in their interaction with government and public authorities, in the health field, in e-commerce transactions, and online generally;

Whereas many individuals are unaware of data protection and privacy laws generally and of specific steps that can be taken to help protect the privacy of personal information online;

Whereas "National Data Privacy Day" constitutes an international collaboration and a nationwide and statewide effort to raise awareness about data privacy and the protection of personal information on the Internet;

Whereas government officials from the United States and Europe, privacy professionals, academics, legal scholars, representatives of international businesses, and others with an interest in data privacy issues are working together on this date to further the discussion about data privacy and protection;

Whereas privacy professionals and educators are being encouraged to take the time to discuss data privacy and protection issues with teens in high schools across the country;

Whereas the recognition of "National Data Privacy Day" will encourage more people nationwide to be aware of data privacy concerns and to take steps to protect their personal information online; and

Whereas January 28, 2009, would be an appropriate day to designate as "National Data Privacy Day": Now, therefore, be it

Resolved, That the House of Representatives—

(1) supports the designation of a "National Data Privacy Day";

(2) encourages State and local governments to observe the day with appropriate activities that promote awareness of data privacy;

(3) encourages privacy professionals and educators to discuss data privacy and protection issues with teens in high schools across the United States; and

(4) encourages individuals across the Nation to be aware of data privacy concerns and to take steps to protect their personal information online.

unfettered discretion to compile detailed information about people can lead to instances of identity theft, increase the prospect of government surveillance, and allow the release of highly sensitive information.[2]

Some First Amendment advocates, however, contend that the push toward regulating informational privacy or data privacy can infringe on First Amendment free-speech rights. Under the First Amendment, even so-called "commercial speech" receives some protection. "Privacy is a popular word, and government attempts to 'protect our privacy' are easy to endorse," writes UCLA law professor Eugene Volokh in an article discussing the First Amendment implications of informational privacy. "The difficulty is that the right to information privacy—my right to control your communication of personally identifiable information about me—is a right to have the government stop you from speaking about me."[3]

Another major issue with respect to privacy concerns its relationship with technology. In one sense, technological advancements have led to the potential for greater invasions of privacy. High-powered cameras with special zoom lenses allow photographers greater ease in tracking people from long distances. Thermal imagers allow the police essentially to see inside a home to detect hot spots and potential illegal drugs.[4] Facial recognition technology potentially offers law enforcement the ability to track terrorists and other dangerous individuals. Technological developments appear to give credence to Justice Brandeis's warning more than 80 years ago in *Olmstead v. United States*:

> The progress of science in furnishing the government with means of espionage is not likely to stop with wire tapping. Ways may someday be developed by which the government, without removing papers from secret drawers, can reproduce them in court, and by which it will be enabled to expose to a jury the most intimate occurrences of the home. Advances in the psychic and related sciences may bring means of exploring

Protecting the Privacy of Social Security Numbers Act of 2009

H. R. 122 (111th Congress) (January 2009)

Congressional Findings:

(1) The inappropriate display, sale, or purchase of Social Security numbers has contributed to a growing range of illegal activities, including fraud, identity theft, and, in some cases, stalking and other violent crimes.

(2) While financial institutions, health care providers, and other entities have often used Social Security numbers to confirm the identity of an individual, the general display to the public, sale, or purchase of these numbers has been used to commit crimes, and also can result in serious invasions of individual privacy.

(3) The Federal Government requires virtually every individual in the United States to obtain and maintain a Social Security number in order to pay taxes, to qualify for Social Security benefits, or to seek employment. An unintended consequence of these requirements is that Social Security numbers have become one of the tools that can be used to facilitate crime, fraud, and invasions of the privacy of the individuals to whom the numbers are assigned. Because the Federal Government created and maintains this system, and because the Federal Government does not permit individuals to exempt themselves from those requirements, it is appropriate for the Federal Government to take steps to stem the abuse of Social Security numbers.

(4) The display, sale, or purchase of Social Security numbers in no way facilitates uninhibited, robust, and wide-open public debate, and restrictions on such display, sale, or purchase would not affect public debate.

(5) No one should seek to profit from the display, sale, or purchase of Social Security numbers in circumstances that create a substantial risk of physical, emotional, or financial harm to the individuals to whom those numbers are assigned.

(6) Consequently, this Act provides each individual that has been assigned a Social Security number some degree of protection from the display, sale, and purchase of that number in any circumstance that might facilitate unlawful conduct.

unexpressed beliefs, thoughts, and emotions."[5] More recently, Justice Stephen Breyer recognized the danger that technology could do to individual personal privacy in his concurring opinion in *Bartnicki v. Vopper* (2001): "The Constitution permits legislatures to respond flexibly to the challenges new technology may pose to the individual's interest in basic personal privacy."[6]

There is another side to the relationship between privacy and technology, however. Just as some technological advancements may infringe on privacy, other such advancements may become a great boon. Scholar Ric Simmons explains that for a century,

millions of individuals ... have begun using everyday technology to increase their privacy.... New technology has also strengthened individual privacy in at least two ways: by enabling governments to target surveillance more effectively, resulting in more narrowly tailored searches; and by enhancing our ability to monitor the conduct of government agents.[7]

He concludes his analysis by noting that "new technologies are not the cause of eroding privacy ... they could be a big part of the cure.[8]

Congress has increased its activity with respect to privacy in recent years. In 2009 alone, measures were introduced to establish a National Data Privacy Day[9], to provide for criminal penalties for the misuse of Social Security numbers in the Protecting the Privacy of Social Security Numbers Act of 2009[10], and to require mobile phones to make a sound when taking photographs, a measure called the Camera Phone Predator Alert Act.[11] This flurry of recent congressional activity is clear evidence that the privacy debate is far from finished. In the years ahead, leaders will continue to debate, discuss, and deliberate on how best to calibrate the need to provide security while also maintaining privacy.

Beginning Legal Research

The goals of each book in the POINT/COUNTERPOINT series are not only to give the reader a basic introduction to a controversial issue affecting society, but also to encourage the reader to explore the issue more fully. This Appendix is meant to serve as a guide to the reader in researching the current state of the law as well as exploring some of the public policy arguments as to why existing laws should be changed or new laws are needed.

Although some sources of law can be found primarily in law libraries, legal research has become much faster and more accessible with the advent of the Internet. This Appendix discusses some of the best starting points for free access to laws and court decisions, but surfing the Web will uncover endless additional sources of information. Before you can research the law, however, you must have a basic understanding of the American legal system.

The most important source of law in the United States is the Constitution. Originally enacted in 1787, the Constitution outlines the structure of our federal government, as well as setting limits on the types of laws that the federal government and state governments can enact. Through the centuries, a number of amendments have added to or changed the Constitution, most notably the first 10 amendments, which collectively are known as the "Bill of Rights" and which guarantee important civil liberties.

Reading the plain text of the Constitution provides little information. For example, the Constitution prohibits "unreasonable searches and seizures" by the police. To understand concepts in the Constitution, it is necessary to look to the decisions of the U.S. Supreme Court, which has the ultimate authority in interpreting the meaning of the Constitution. For example, the U.S. Supreme Court's 2001 decision in *Kyllo v. United States* held that scanning the outside of a person's house using a heat sensor to determine whether the person is growing marijuana is an unreasonable search—if it is done without first getting a search warrant from a judge. Each state also has its own constitution and a supreme court that is the ultimate authority on its meaning.

Also important are the written laws, or "statutes," passed by the U.S. Congress and the individual state legislatures. As with constitutional provisions, the U.S. Supreme Court and the state supreme courts are the ultimate authorities in interpreting the meaning of federal and state laws, respectively. However, the U.S. Supreme Court might find that a state law violates the U.S. Constitution, and a state supreme court might find that a state law violates either the state or U.S. Constitution.

APPENDIX ||||▷

Not every controversy reaches either the U.S. Supreme Court or the state supreme courts, however. Therefore, the decisions of other courts are also important. Trial courts hear evidence from both sides and make a decision, while appeals courts review the decisions made by trial courts. Sometimes rulings from appeals courts are appealed further to the U.S. Supreme Court or the state supreme courts.

Lawyers and courts refer to statutes and court decisions through a formal system of citations. Use of these citations reveals which court made the decision or which legislature passed the statute, and allows one to quickly locate the statute or court case online or in a law library. For example, the Supreme Court case *Brown v. Board of Education* has the legal citation 347 U.S. 483 (1954). At a law library, this 1954 decision can be found on page 483 of volume 347 of the U.S. Reports, which are the official collection of the Supreme Court's decisions. On the following page, you will find samples of all the major kinds of legal citation.

Finding sources of legal information on the Internet is relatively simple thanks to "portal" sites such as findlaw.com and lexisone.com, which allow the user to access a variety of constitutions, statutes, court opinions, law review articles, news articles, and other useful sources of information. For example, findlaw.com offers access to all Supreme Court decisions since 1893. Other useful sources of information include gpo.gov, which contains a complete copy of the U.S. Code, and thomas.loc.gov, which offers access to bills pending before Congress, as well as recently passed laws. Of course, the Internet changes every second of every day, so it is best to do some independent searching.

Of course, many people still do their research at law libraries, some of which are open to the public. For example, some state governments and universities offer the public access to their law collections. Law librarians can be of great assistance, as even experienced attorneys need help with legal research from time to time.

Common Citation Forms

Source of Law	Sample Citation	Notes
U.S. Supreme Court	*Employment Division v. Smith*, 485 U.S. 660 (1988)	The U.S. Reports is the official record of Supreme Court decisions. There is also an unofficial Supreme Court ("S. Ct.") reporter.
U.S. Court of Appeals	*United States v. Lambert*, 695 F.2d 536 (11th Cir.1983)	Appellate cases appear in the Federal Reporter, designated by "F." The 11th Circuit has jurisdiction in Alabama, Florida, and Georgia.
U.S. District Court	*Carillon Importers, Ltd. v. Frank Pesce Group, Inc.*, 913 F.Supp. 1559 (S.D.Fla.1996)	Federal trial-level decisions are reported in the Federal Supplement ("F. Supp."). Some states have multiple federal districts; this case originated in the Southern District of Florida.
U.S. Code	Thomas Jefferson Commemoration Commission Act, 36 U.S.C., §149 (2002)	Sometimes the popular names of legislation—names with which the public may be familiar—are included with the U.S. Code citation.
State Supreme Court	*Sterling v. Cupp*, 290 Ore. 611, 614, 625 P.2d 123, 126 (1981)	The Oregon Supreme Court decision is reported in both the state's reporter and the Pacific regional reporter.
State Statute	Pennsylvania Abortion Control Act of 1982, 18 Pa. Cons. Stat. 3203-3220 (1990)	States use many different citation formats for their statutes.

Cases

Olmstead v. United States, 277 U.S. 438 (1928)

The U.S. Supreme Court ruled that government officials did not violate the Fourth Amendment when they wiretapped the conversations of suspected bootlegger Roy Olmstead. The majority of the Court found that the Fourth Amendment did not extend to wiretaps because there was no physical invasion. The Supreme Court overturned this rationale in *Katz v. United States* (1967).

NAACP v. Alabama, 357 U.S. 449 (1958)

In this case, the U.S. Supreme Court ruled that the state of Alabama could not force the National Association for the Advancement of Colored People (NAACP), a civil rights group, from disclosing its private membership lists.

Mapp v. Ohio, 367 U.S. 463 (1961)

In this decision, the U.S. Supreme Court determined that the police in Cleveland, Ohio, violated the Fourth Amendment when they rummaged through the house of Dollree Mapp. The Court also ruled that the illegally obtained evidence had to be excluded, and extended this exclusionary rule to the states.

Griswold v. Connecticut, 381 U.S. 479 (1965)

The U.S. Supreme Court found that the state of Connecticut could not intrude into the sphere of marital privacy by criminalizing the use of contraceptives. The case is best known for the Court's ruling that the Constitution protects a right to privacy, even though the term is not used in the Bill of Rights.

Katz v. United States, 389 U.S. 347 (1967)

In this decision, the U.S. Supreme Court found that government officials violated the Fourth Amendment rights of gambler Charles Katz when they "bugged" public telephones without first obtaining a warrant. The case extended Fourth Amendment rights even to certain public places when there was a "reasonable expectation of privacy"—a concept developed by Justice John Marshall Harlan II in his concurring opinion.

Dietemann v. Time, 449 F.2d 245 (9th Cir. 1971)

A federal appeals court ruled that reporters for *Life* invaded the privacy rights of a supposed healer when they used a hidden camera to photograph the man in his home. The case demonstrates the principle that the media is not entitled to special constitutional protection for its newsgathering activities.

Galella v. Onassis, 487 F.2d 986 (2nd Cir. 1973)

In this decision, a federal appeals court ruled that photographer Ronald Galella could be prohibited from coming in close contact with former first lady Jacqueline Kennedy Onassis and her children. The court determined that Galella's activities were beyond the reasonable bounds of newsgathering.

Cox Broadcasting Co. v. Cohn, 420 U.S. 469 (1975)

The U.S. Supreme Court ruled that a reporter could not be punished in a civil suit or a criminal one for revealing the name of a juvenile rape victim when he discovered the victim's name from an official record.

Zurcher v. Stanford Daily, 436 U.S. 547 (1978)

The U.S. Supreme Court upheld the search of a student collegiate newspaper, reasoning that the government can conduct searches of third parties who are innocent as long as it has probable cause to believe there is evidence on the premises that will assist law enforcement in its investigation. In response to this decision, Congress passed the Privacy Protection Act of 1980, which gave more protection to the media from such searches.

Desnick v. American Broadcasting Co., 44 F.3d 1345 (7th Cir. 1995)

A federal appeals court ruled that neither a television station nor its employees were liable for their actions in uncovering fraud being committed in an eye clinic that allegedly encouraged people to have unnecessary medical procedures.

Lawrence v. Texas, 559 U.S. 538 (2003)

In this decision, the U.S. Supreme Court struck down a Texas statute that criminalized private sex acts between consenting adults.

Terms and Concepts

Appropriation

Biometrics

Common law

False-light invasion of privacy

Fifth Amendment

First Amendment

Fourth Amendment

Intrusion

Newsgathering

Paparazzi

Public disclosure of private facts

Reasonable expectation of privacy

Surveillance

Tort

Upskirting

Video voyeurism

Introduction: An Overview of the Right to Privacy

1 *Olmstead v. United States*, 277 U.S. 438, 478 (1928) (J. Brandeis, dissenting).

2 Jim Harper, "Understanding Privacy—and the Real Threats to It," Policy Analysis, Cato Institute, August 4, 2004.

3 Sissela Bok, *On The Ethics of Concealment & Revelation* (1983). Reproduced in Richard C. Turkington and Anita L. Allen, *Privacy Law: Cases and Materials.* St. Paul, Minn.: West Group 2002, 75.

4 Ken Gormley, "One Hundred Years of Privacy," 1992 *Wisconsin Law Review* 1335, 1339 (1992).

5 *Ibid.*, 1340.

6 Samuel Warren and Louis Brandeis, "The Right to Privacy," 4 *Harvard Law Review* 193 (1890).

7 *Ibid.*, 196.

8 *Ibid.*, 198.

9 *Ibid.*, 195.

10 *Ibid.*

11 William L. Prosser, "Privacy," 48 California Law Review 383 (1960).

12 *Restatement (Second) of Torts*, §652(D).

13 *Cox Broadcasting Co. v. Cohn*, 420 U.S. 469 (1975).

14 *Restatement (Second) of Torts*, §652(E).

15 *Restatement (Second) of Torts*, §652(C).

16 *NAACP v. Alabama*, 357 U.S. 449 (1958).

17 *Mapp v Ohio*, 367 U.S. 643, 656 (1961).

18 Otis H. Stephens and Richard H. Glenn, *Unreasonable Searches and Seizures: Rights and Liberties Under Law.* Santa Barbara, Calif.: ABC-CLIO, 2006, 241.

19 American Civil Liberties Union, "Surveillance under the Patriot Act," March 3, 2003. http://www.aclu.org/safefree/general/17326res20030403.html.

20 *Griswold v. Connecticut*, 381 U.S. 479, 484 (1965).

21 *Ibid.*, (J. Goldberg, concurring).

22 *Lawrence v. Texas*, 539 U.S. 558 (2003).

23 Family Educational Rights and Privacy Act, U.S. Code 20 (1974), 20 U.S.C. 1232g.

24 Right to Financial Privacy Act, U.S. Code 12 (1978), 12 U.S.C. 3401.

25 *Zurcher v. Stanford Daily*, 436 U.S. 547 (1978).

26 Electronic Communications Privacy Act, U.S. Code 18 (1986), 18 U.S.C. 2707.

27 Video Privacy Protection of 1988, U.S. Code 18 (1988), 18 U.S.C. 2710.

28 Driver Privacy Protection Act, U.S. Code 18 (1994), 18 U.S.C. 2721-2725.

Point: Governmental Surveillance Often Infringes on Individuals' Fourth Amendment Rights

1 Ellen Alderman and Caroline Kennedy, *The Right to Privacy.* New York: Alfred A. Knopf, 1995, xv.

2 Jim Harper, "Understanding Privacy—and the Real Threats to It," Policy Analysis, Cato Institute, August 4, 2004, No. 520, p. 2.

3 *Olmstead v. United States*, 277 U.S. 438 (1928).

4 *Olmstead v. United States*, 277 U.S. 438, 477 (1928) (J. Brandeis, dissenting).

5 *Katz v. United States*, 389 U.S. 347 (1967).

6 *Ibid.*, 353.

7 *Ibid.*, 358.

8 *Berger v. New York*, 388 U.S. 41, 63 (1967).

9 Electronic Privacy Information Center, Comments to Department of Homeland Security on Docket No. DHS-2007-0076: January 15, 2008, p. 9. http://epic.org/privacy/surveillance/epic_cctv_011508.pdf.

10 Jeremy Brown, "Privacy: Pan, Tilt, Zoom: Regulating the Use of Video Surveillance of Public Places," 23 *Berkeley Technology Law Journal* 755, 773 (2008).

11 National Center for Victims of Crime, "Video Voyeurism Laws," July 2005. http://www.ncvc.org/ncvc/AGP.Net/Components/documentViewer/Download.aspxnz?DocumentID=40459.

12 Kristin Beasley, "Up-Skirt and Other Dirt: Why Cell Phone Cameras and Other Technologies Require a New Approach to Protecting Personal Privacy in Public Places," 31 *Southern Illinois University Law Journal* 69, 79 (2006).

13 *Ibid.*, 80.

14 Electronic Privacy Information Center, Comments to Department of Homeland Security, 9–10.

15 Marc Rotenberg, "Joint Public Oversight Hearing, Committee on the Judiciary on Public Works and the Environment," City Council of the District of Columbia, June 13, 2002. http://epic.org/privacy/surveillance/testimony_061302.html.

16 Noam Biale, "Expert Findings on Surveillance Cameras: What Criminologists and Others Studying Cameras Have Found," American Civil Liberties Union. http://www.aclu.org/privacy/35775res20080625.html.

17 James Risen and Eric Lichtblau, "Bush Lets U.S. Spy on Callers Without Courts," New York Times, December 16, 2005.

18 H.R. 6304.

19 American Civil Liberties Union, "Why the FISA Amendments Act Is Unconstitutional," ACLU.org, July 10, 2008. http://www.aclu.org/images/nsaspying/asset_upload_file578_35950.pdf.

20 Ibid.

21 ACLU news release, "ACLU Sues Over Unconstitutional New Dragnet Wiretapping Law," July 10, 2008. http://www.aclu.org/safefree/nsaspying/35942prs20080710.html.

Counterpoint: Modern Surveillance Provides Necessary Security and Does Not Violate the Fourth Amendment

1 The 9/11 Commission Report. New York: W.W. Norton, 2004, 386.

2 Ibid., xvi.

3 Julie Hilden, "The ACLU on Surveillance: Despite Its Overarching Assessment of How Monitoring Harms Privacy, a New Report Fails to Offer Constructive Solutions," Findlaw Writ, January 21, 2003. http://writ.news.findlaw.com/scripts/printer_friendly.pl?page=/hilden/20030121.html.

4 Max Guirguis, "Electronic Visual Surveillance and the Reasonable Expectation of Privacy," 9 Journal of Technology Law & Policy 143, 147 (2004).

5 Ibid.

6 Richard Posner, "Surveillance, Privacy and the Law," 75 University of Chicago Law Review 245, 247 (2008).

7 United States v. Torres, 751 F.2d 875, 883 (7th Cir. 1984).

8 James Cannon, "Winning Framework to Implement Surveillance Technologies to Enhance the Police and Community Partnership," Journal of California Law Enforcement 42 (2008), 18.

9 Michelle Lirtzman, "Surveillance Cameras Win Broad Support," ABC News, July 29, 2007. http://abcnews.go.com/print?id=3422372.

10 James A. Baker, testifying before the Senate Committee on the Judiciary, on September 25, 2007. http://judiciary.senate.gov/hearings/testimony.cfm?renderforprint=1&id=2942&wit_id=6669.

11 Posner, "Surveillance, Privacy and the Law," 252.

12 Ibid.

13 H.R. 6304 (110th Cong.).

Point: Increasingly Intrusive Newsgathering Efforts Threaten Privacy Rights

1 Samuel D. Warren and Louis Brandeis, "The Right to Privacy," 4 Harvard Law Review 192, 196 (1890).

2 Ibid., 195.

3 J. Thomas McCarthy, The Rights of Publicity and Privacy, vol. 1, 2nd ed. St. Paul, Minn.: Thomson West, 2008, 18–21.

4 Warren and Brandeis, "The Right to Privacy," 195.

5 Restatement (Second) of Torts, §652(B).

6 Jeffrey Fleischmann, "French authorities detain 7 paparazzi, consider charges," Philadelphia Inquirer, August 31, 1997.

7 Dan Morain, "2 State Senators Back Limits on Paparazzi," Los Angeles Times, September 3, 1997.

8 David M. Halbfinger and Allison Hope Weiner, "As Paparazzi Push Ever Harder, Stars Seek a Way to Push Back," New York Times, June 9, 2005.

9 Ibid.

10 Mark Schwed, "Look Who's Stalking: Aggressive Photographers Are the Focus of a Celebrity Fight to Stop the 'Stalkerazzi'—Before Someone Gets Hurt," Palm Beach Post, September 1, 2005.

11 Dietemann v. Time, 449 F.2d 245 (9th Cir. 1971).

12 Ibid., 248.

13 Ibid., 249.

14 *Galella v. Onassis,* 487 F.3d 986, 992 (2nd Cir. 1973).
15 *Ibid.,* 996.
16 *Wolfson v. Lewis,* 924 F.Supp. 1413, 1420 (E.D. Pa. 1996).
17 *Ibid.,* 1433.
18 *Calif. Civ. Code* § 1708.8(b).
19 *Ibid.*
20 Alan Kato Ku, "Talk Is Cheap, But a Picture Is Worth a Thousand Words: Privacy Rights in the Era of Camera Phone Technology," 45 *Santa Clara Law Review* 679, 692–693 (2005).
21 *State v. Glas,* 54 P.3d 147, 150 (Wash. 2002).
22 *Ibid.,* 151.
23 Ku, "Talk Is Cheap," 705–706.
24 *Olmstead v. United States,* 277 U.S. 438, 478 (1928) (J. Brandeis dissent).

Counterpoint: The Constitution Protects Even Aggressive Newsgathering

1 John Seigenthaler and David L. Hudson Jr., "Going Undercover," *Quill,* March 1, 1997.
2 C. Thomas Dienes, "The Media's Intrusion on Privacy," 67 *George Washington Law Review* 1139, 1142 (1999).
3 Jerry Thompson, *My Life in the Klan.* Nashville, Tenn.: Routledge Hill Press, 1988.
4 *Branzburg v. Hayes,* 408 U.S. 665, 681 (1972).
5 Erwin Chemerinsky, "Protect the Press: A First Amendment Safeguard for Safeguarding Aggressive Newsgathering," 33 *University of Richmond Law Review* 1143, 1144 (2000).
6 Chemerinsky at p. 1160.
7 Dienes, "The Media's Intrusion on Privacy," 1139, 1143.
8 John W. Wade, "The Tort Liability of Investigative Reporters," 37 *Vanderbilt Law Review* 301, 346 (1984).
9 *Desnick v. American Broadcasting Co.,* 44 F.3d 1345 (7th Cir. 1995).
10 *Northside Realty Associates Inc. v. United States,* 605 F.2d 1348, 1355 (5th Cir. 1979).
11 *New York Times Co. v. Sullivan,* 376 U.S. 254, 270 (1964).
12 *Ibid.,* 280.
13 *Ibid.,* 279.

14 Paul A. LeBel, "The Constitutional Interest in Getting the News: Toward a First Amendment Protection from Tort Liability for Surreptitious Newsgathering," 4 *William & Mary Bill of Rights Journal* 1145, 1147 (1996).
15 *Ibid.,* 1154.
16 *Ibid.,* 1155.
17 Kathleen Kirby, "Freedom of Information: Law and the Newsgathering Process," Radio-Television News Directors Association. http://www.rtnda.org/pages/media_items/law-and-the-newsgathering-process186.php.

Point: Employees Need and Deserve Greater Privacy Protections in the Workplace

1 Morey Stettner, "More Firms Will Eye Blogs, E-Mail in '08," *Investor's Business Daily,* December 31, 2007.
2 *Ibid.*
3 Joseph Migga Kizza and Jackline Ssanyu, "Workplace Surveillance," in *Electronic Monitoring in the Workplace: Controversies and Solutions,* John Weckert, ed. Hershey, Pa.: Idea Group Publishing: 2005, 1–18, 12–14.
4 *Ibid.,* 12.
5 *Ibid.,* 13.
6 David Zweig, "Beyond Privacy and Fairness Concerns: Examining Psychological Boundary Violations as a Consequence of Electronic Performance Monitoring," in *Electronic Monitoring in the Workplace: Controversies and Solutions,* John Weckert, ed. Hershey, Pa.: Idea Group Publishing: 2005, 101–122.
7 *Ibid.,* 113.
8 *O'Connor v. Ortega,* 480 U.S. 709, 717 (1987).
9 *Avila v. Valentin-Maldonado,* 2008 U.S. Dist. LEXIS 21823 (D. PR) (March 19, 2008) at pp. 35–36.
10 *Quon v. Arch Wireless Operating Co.,* 529 F.3d 892 (9th Cir. 2008).
11 William R. Corbett, "The Need for a Revitalized Common Law of the Workplace," 69 *Brooklyn Law Review* 91, 102 (2003).
12 *Ibid.,* 103.
13 Frederick Lane, *The Naked Employee.* New York: Amacom, 2003, 241.

Counterpoint: Employees Have Limited Expectations of Privacy in the Workplace

1 "2007 Electronic Monitoring & Surveillance Report," American Management Association, February 28, 2008. http://press.amanet.org/press-releases/177/2007-electronic-monitoring-surveillance-survey/.

2 *United States v. Gonzalez,* 328 F.3d 543 (9th Cir. 2003).

3 *United States v. Reilly,* 2002 U.S. Dist. LEXIS 9865 (S.D.N.Y.) (June 3, 2002), p. 11.

4 *Ibid.,* 12.

5 *Smyth v. The Pillsbury Company,* 914 F.Supp. 97 (E.D. Pa. 1996).

6 *Ibid.,* 101.

7 *Ibid.*

8 Stephen J. Stine, "Internet monitoring: Why keep an eye on surfing and e-mailing in the office?" Virginia Employment Law Letter, May 2007.

9 *Ibid.*

10 Quoted in "2007 Electronic Monitoring & Surveillance Report," American Management Association.

11 Marilyn Gardner, "Why go to the mall when you can shop at work," *Christian Science Monitor,* December 10, 2007.

12 Suzanne Choney, "Web at work: Not YourSpace," MSNBC.com, March 27, 2008.

13 "2007 Electronic Monitoring & Surveillance Report," American Management Association.

14 Jennifer Dudley, "Cyberslacking is the new workplace sport," *Daily Telegraph,* April 26, 2006.

Conclusion: The Future of Privacy Rights

1 "Privacy Today." Privacy Rights Clearinghouse. http://www.privacyrights.org/ar/Privacy-IssuesList.htm#t.

2 Neil D. Richards, "Reconciling Data Privacy and the First Amendment," 52 *UCLA Law Review* 1149, 1158 (2005).

3 Eugene Volokh, "Freedom of Speech and Information Privacy: The Troubling Implications of a Right to Stop People From Speaking About You," 52 *Stanford Law Review* 1049, 1050–1051 (2000).

4 *Kyllo v. United States,* 533 U.S. 27 (2001).

5 *Olmstead v. United States,* 277 U.S. 438, 478 (1928) (J. Brandeis, dissenting).

6 *Bartnicki v. Vopper,* 532 U.S. 514, 541 (2001) (J. Breyer, concurring).

7 Ric Simmons, "Why 2007 Is Not Like 1984: A Broader Perspective on Technology's Effect on Privacy and Fourth Amendment Jurisprudence," 97 *Journal of Criminal Law & Criminology* 531 (2007).

8 *Ibid.*

9 H. Res. 31 (111th Cong.) (January 26, 2009).

10 H.R. 122 (111th Cong.) (January 6, 2009).

11 H.R. 414 (11th Cong.) (January 9, 2009).

RESOURCES ||||▷

Books and Articles

Agre, Philip, and Marc Rotenberg, eds. *Technology and Privacy: The New Landscape.* Cambridge, Mass.: MIT Press, 1997.

Alderman, Ellen, and Caroline Kennedy. *The Right to Privacy.* New York: Alfred A. Knopf, 1995.

Allen, Anita. "Lying to Protect Privacy," 44 *Villanova Law Review* 161 (1999).

Beasley, Kristin, "Up-Skirt and Other Dirt: Why Cell Phone Cameras and Other Technologies Require a New Approach to Protecting Personal Privacy in Public Places," 31 *Southern Illinois University Law Journal* 69 (2006).

Brill, Alida. *Nobody's Business: The Paradoxes of Privacy.* Reading, Mass.: Addison-Wesley, 1990.

Brin, David. *The Transparent Society: Will Technology Force Us to Choose Between Privacy and Freedom?* Reading, Mass.: Addison-Wesley, 1998.

Brown, Jeremy, "Privacy: Pan, Tilt, Zoom: Regulating the Use of Video Surveillance of Public Places," 23 *Berkeley Technology Law Journal* 755 (2008).

Chemerinsky, Erwin. "Protect the Press: A First Amendment Safeguard for Safeguarding Aggressive Newsgathering," 33 *University of Richmond Law Review* 1143 (2000).

Corbett, William R. "The Need for a Revitalized Common Law of the Workplace," 69 *Brooklyn Law Review* 91 (2003).

Dienes, C. Thomas. "The Media's Intrusion on Privacy," 67 *George Washington Law Review* 1139 (1999).

Etzioni, Amitai. *The Limits of Privacy.* New York: Basic Books, 1999.

Gavison, Ruth. "Privacy and the Limits of Law," 89 *Yale Law Journal* 421 (1980).

Gormley, Ken. "One Hundred Years of Privacy," *Wisconsin Law Review* 1335 (1992).

Hentoff, Nat. *The War on the Bill of Rights and the Gathering Resistance.* New York: Seven Stories Press, 2003.

Hofstadter, Samuel H., and George Horowitz. *The Right of Privacy.* New York: Central Book, 1964.

Kalven, Harry Jr. "Privacy in Tort Law—Were Warren and Brandeis Wrong?" 31 *Law & Contemporary Legal Problems* 326 (1966).

Lane, Frederick. *The Naked Employee.* New York: Amacom, 2003.

LeBel, Paul A. "The Constitutional Interest in Getting the News: Toward a First Amendment Protection from Tort Liability for Surreptitious News-gathering," 4 *William & Mary Bill of Rights Journal* 1145 (1996).

Lebron, D.W. "The Right to Privacy's Place in the Intellectual History of Tort Law." 41 *Case Western Law Review* 769 (1991).

Ku, Alan Kato. "Talk is Cheap, But a Picture Is Worth a Thousand Words: Privacy Rights in the Era of Camera Phone Technology," 35 *Santa Clara Law Review* 679 (2005).

Miller, Arthur. *The Assault on Privacy.* Ann Arbor: University of Michigan, 1971.

Noble, June, and William Noble. *The Private Me.* New York: Delacorte Press, 1980.

Packard, Vance. *The Naked Society.* New York: Pocket Books, 1964.

Posner, Richard. "Surveillance, Privacy and the Law," 75 *University of Chicago Law Review* 245 (2008).

Post, Robert C. "The Social Foundations of Privacy: Community and Self in the Common Law Tort," 77 *California Law Review* 957 (1989).

Prosser, William L. "Privacy," 48 *California Law Review* 383 (1960).

Richards, Neil D. "Reconciling Data Privacy and the First Amendment," 52 *UCLA Law Review* 1149 (2005).

Rosen, Jeffrey. *The Unwanted Gaze: The Destruction of Privacy in America.* New York: Random House, 2000.

Rubenfeld, Jed. "The Right of Privacy," 102 *Harvard Law Review* 737 (1990).

Rule, James B. *Private Lives and Public Surveillance.* London: Allen Lane, 1973.

Schoeman, Ferdinand David. *Privacy and Social Freedom.* New York: Cambridge University Press, 1992.

RESOURCES ||||▷

Simmons, Ric. "Why 2007 Is Not Like 1984: A Broader Perspective on Technology's Effect on Privacy and Fourth Amendment Jurisprudence," 97 *Journal of Criminal Law & Criminology* 531 (2007).

Solove, Daniel J. *Understanding Privacy.* Boston: Harvard University Press, 2008.

Staples, William G. *The Culture of Surveillance: Discipline and Social Control in the United States.* New York: St. Martin's Press, 1997.

Stephens, Otis H., and Richard H. Glenn. *Unreasonable Searches and Seizures: Rights and Liberties Under Law.* Santa Barbara, Calif.: ABC-CLIO, 2006.

Turkington, Richard C., and Anita L. Allen. *Privacy Law: Cases and Materials.* St. Paul, Minn.: West Group, 2002.

Volokh, Eugene. "Freedom of Speech and Information Privacy: The Troubling Implications of a Right to Stop People from Speaking About You," 52 *Stanford Law Review* 1049 (2000).

Warren, Samuel F., and Louis Brandeis, "The Right to Privacy," 4 *Harvard Law Review* 193 (1890).

Westin, Alan F. "Science, Privacy and Freedom," 66 *Columbia Law Review* 1003 (1966).

Westin, Alan F. *Privacy and Freedom.* New York: Atheneum, 1967.

Web Sites

American Civil Liberties Union (ACLU)
http://www.aclu.org/privacy/
This broad-based civil liberties group is devoted, among other things, to protecting privacy. Its Web site has a special section pertaining to privacy issues.

Center for Democracy & Technology
http://www.cdt.org/
This group says that it "works to promote democratic values and constitutional liberties in the digital age" and "seeks practical solutions to enhance free expression and privacy in global communications technologies."

Electronic Frontier Foundation (EFF)
http://www.eff.org
This organization is the self-described "leading civil liberties group defending your rights in the digital world."

Electronic Privacy Information Center (EPIC)

http://epic.org/

This Washington, D.C.-based group has an impressive Web site that details various threats to privacy. The EPIC site contains many materials pertaining to government surveillance and technology.

The ePolicy Institute

http://www.epolicyinstitute.com/

This management-rights-based group examines electronic security and privacy from the perspective of businesses.

Privacy Foundation

http://www.privacyfoundation.org/

This organization, located in Denver, provides much information on student privacy, workplace privacy, financial privacy, and other issues.

Privacy Rights Clearinghouse

http://www.privacyrights.org/

This site presents an impressive overview of different privacy issues, including a section called "Privacy Today" that lists 21 major privacy issues.

PICTURE CREDITS ⫸

DAVID L. HUDSON JR. is a First Amendment Scholar at the First Amendment Center at Vanderbilt University. He teaches law classes at Middle Tennessee State University, Nashville School of Law, and Vanderbilt Law School. He is the author or co-author of more than 20 books, including several in the POINT/COUNTERPOINT series.

ALAN MARZILLI, M.A., J.D., lives in Birmingham, Ala., and is a program associate with Advocates for Human Potential, Inc., a research and consulting firm based in Sudbury, Mass., and Albany, N.Y. He primarily works on developing training and educational materials for agencies of the federal government on topics such as housing, mental health policy, employment, and transportation. He has spoken on mental health issues in 30 states, the District of Columbia, and Puerto Rico; his work has included training mental health administrators, nonprofit management and staff, and people with mental illnesses and their families on a wide variety of topics, including effective advocacy, community-based mental health services, and housing. He has written several handbooks and training curricula that are used nationally—as far away as the territory of Guam. He managed statewide and national mental health advocacy programs and worked for several public interest lobbying organizations while studying law at Georgetown University. He has written more than a dozen books, including numerous titles in the POINT/COUNTERPOINT series.